W9-BUF-513

Words of Support for

However Long the Night:
Making Meaning in a Time of Crisis

However Long the Night is a perfect title for a wonderful book. It is about leadership in crisis that chose a path of intelligence, reflection, compassion, and silence in the face of harmful and disheartening opposition. It documents what communal and relational leadership looks like. It is a feminine form of leadership that the world needs desperately. Beautifully personal in tone and style, this book offers a glimpse of how high integrity and conscious leadership can bring reconciliation into the world. In the end, this story makes us grateful that there are women religious always at our side as proof of concept that God is present.
-- *Peter Block, Author,* An Other Kingdom

The Leadership Conference of Women Religious has set the new gold standard for "speaking truth to power." It is an honor to be in the presence of these women and to hear their story first hand.
-- *The Rev. Cynthia Bourgeault, Episcopal priest, author, and retreat leader*

In an era of polarization, conflict, and disrespect, the timeliness of *However Long the Night* could not be more relevant. With concise, transparent, respectful, and honest dialogue the authors lay open a needed paradigm shift based on truth and trust. Women religious have always desired to be "of service" to others and this text is just one more fine example of their service to and for the common good of our country and our church.
-- *Patricia Chappell, SNDdeN, Executive Director, Pax Christi USA*

If anything gives evidence of the breadth and depth of the renewal and transformation of the lives of women religious in the United States, this volume is it. These essays, detailing LCWR's experience in responding to a doctrinal assessment and mandate for reform, offer a stunning, compelling, inspiring, prophetic witness to an alternate, contemplative way of dealing with misunderstanding, conflict, and disapproval. In a country beset by violent language, lack of civility, intolerance, and polarization, the leaders of LCWR model a path marked by fidelity to prayer and deep listening, commitment to dialogue and respectful relationship, and undying hope for mutuality and communion. Humility, strength, honesty, and integrity characterize their voices.
-- *Constance FitzGerald, OCD, Baltimore Carmel*

LCWR's response to the CDF doctrinal investigation offered prophetic testimony to the demands of Gospel fidelity. Its prayerful response to an often dysfunctional exercise of authority navigated between the twin temptations to petty defiance and resigned acquiescence. These reflections by LCWR leadership represent nothing less than a primer in a profoundly practical ecclesiology. LCWR's commitment to dialogue with integrity and attentiveness to the primacy of conscience reflect its deep roots in the teaching of the Second Vatican Council. Its commitment to ecclesial discernment and the synodality of a "listening church" anticipated the bracing ecclesial vision of Pope Francis. This volume deserves to be prayerfully studied by all those called to lead in times of conflict and turmoil.

-- *Richard Gaillardetz, Joseph Professor of Catholic Systematic Theology, Boston College*

To have begun this book with pre-emptive "righteous indignation" (at "the opposition"), and finished contrite and deeply enlightened, represents the beginning of a much-needed conversion in this reader. Articulating the assumptions of a confrontational culture cannot be authentic Christianity; and this book shows what is needed when personal bias appears so Godly and other people so wrong-headed.

The whole tenor of the LCWR approach to ecclesiastical censure was not simply strategic nonviolence but a paradigm of respectful listening, deep self-examination, and principled articulation of religious faith. The dignity of each party was maintained and an impasse became a way forward. There is practical wisdom and deep virtue in these pages. Many men badly need the attitudinal shift described here. It is the only way to transform self-righteousness into true righteousness. Here is a pearl of great price.

-- *Anthony J. Gittins, CSSp, PhD, Emeritus Professor of Theology and Culture at Catholic Theological Union*

How grateful we are for Catholic sisters who weathered adversity with grace and modeled the civility, discipline, integrity, and humility so vital to the church and to society. We cherish the lessons we learn from the stories of sisters and admire their boldness as they turn moments of tension into opportunities for growth.

– *Amy Rauenhorst Goldman, CEO & Chair, GHR Foundation*

This extraordinary book falls like a gentle rain upon these parched times of escalating polarization. It brings forth wisdom gleaned during an intensely painful situation and generously shares what the sisters have learned. It offers a process that others in a conflictual situation can use. Call on the Spirit! Contemplate, listen, dialogue, discern! Stay at the table so long as integrity is not compromised! By enfolding a narrative of discord into a broader and deeper narrative of a tough spiritual journey, this book dramatically narrates a form of leadership that can light a path to peace with justice.
-- *Elizabeth Johnson, CSJ, Distinguished Professor of Theology at Fordham University*

The story of the Vatican's investigation of the Leadership Conference of Women Religious, the LCWR's response, and the church's final support for this vital group is one of the most important Catholic stories of our time. Stung by some very public critiques by the Vatican's Congregation for the Doctrine of the Faith, the members of this incredible organization responded with grace, courage, and hope. This dramatic story of power, discernment, hope, pain, and, ultimately, faith, should be required reading for anyone seeking to understand the Catholic church in our age.
-- *James Martin, SJ, author of* Jesus: A Pilgrimage *and consultor to the Vatican's Secretariat for Communication*

Although moved to tears a few times, I also found the sisters' essays extremely instructive. The insights and courage brought about through suffering, prayer, and contemplative dialogue birth hope that it is possible to find a way through seemingly impossible, complicated, and long-standing misunderstandings. They reveal the inner and outer work necessary when two very different cultures clash, but also commit to pursue mutual understanding to achieve communion. This is a book to read over and over as it witnesses how it is possible to recognize the Spirit's call to be a prophetic presence in the most unexpected place.
-- *Joyce Meyer, PBVM, International Liaison for* Global Sisters Report

This volume of essays by the women who led US women religious through the negotiation of the mandate that followed the devastating "Doctrinal Assessment of the Leadership Conference of Women Religious" into a reaffirmation of the value of religious life, the validity of the response to Vatican II of US women religious, and the integrity in faith and action of LCWR, is sheer gift. It is a gift, first of all, because the authors have chosen to relive the pain of these deeply negative experiences in order to share with us, the wider community of religious and laity in the church, the path they forged through these traumatic experiences to deep spiritual peace, steadfastness in vocation and ministry, increased legitimate autonomy as women in the church, and ongoing fidelity to the gift of religious life to the church and the world. It is a gift because of its content, its modeling of how to not only survive injustice and persecution but how to live into it and through it in courage, hope, solidarity, and paschal self-surrender and even enable others to discover their own capacity for something better. And it is a gift because it finally responds to some of the deepest anxieties of religious and laity, Catholics and others, who wondered, through the long silence of the process, what was really going on and feared that intimidation would rob us all of the strong, clear voice of women religious in the church. The answers are here now for all to read, and hopefully to incorporate into our own experience of vocation and response.

-- *Sandra Schneiders, IHM, professor emerita of New Testament studies and spirituality, Jesuit School of Theology/Graduate Theological Union, Berkeley, California*

However Long the Night is a provocative shared memoir of a challenging moment in the history of LCWR. Don't read it as a history, but a work of art to be engaged. Its varied perspectives reveal a story in distinct and sometimes surprising ways, and the questions at the end of each essay invite learning from our own stories as well. At core the chapters speak of discernment, of being faithful to God's call when distractions and temptations could lead one otherwise. Congratulations to LCWR leadership past and present for bringing this story to life.

-- *Thomas H. Smolich, SJ, International Director of the Jesuit Refugee Service*

The story of LCWR's journey through the doctrinal assessment is one of astonishing integrity and compassion. Learning how women religious moved through this most public and personally painful experience is a masterclass in spiritual maturity and organizational strategy.

For Millennial readers such as myself, to learn that crisis-management meetings started with 45 minutes of silence, for example, is a practical call to a different way of being in leadership. Now that our country is deeply polarized and perplexed as to how to heal, *However Long the Night* teaches us how to lead with integrity, stand together in trust, and forever center the vision of a world transformed -- even when our hearts are breaking.

This book is the ultimate affirmation of the faithfulness and authenticity of LCWR and a source of practical inspiration for anyone navigating the travails of conflict.

-- *Casper ter Kuile, Harvard Ministry Innovation Fellow*

I hold the witness and vision of the Leadership Conference of Women Religious in profound esteem. Their communities are forces for spiritual renewal in our spiritually hungry world. They have navigated a period of crisis with prophetic imagination and courage. As they, with this book, offer their learnings to our larger cultural moment of crisis, they continue to model the very meaning of living tradition.
-- *Krista Tippett, Host of "On Being" and Curator of "The Civil Conversations Project"*

I have no hesitation in stating that this is the best leadership book I have yet to read on how to lead through a crisis-laden time and emerge with one's integrity, community, capacity, and faith stronger for the experience. Frequently now, leaders must navigate through conflicts with those who would overwhelm them and take away their power. These situations challenge leaders to their very core; the usual response is to meet aggression with aggression and thus only increase the conflict and dysfunction.

Here is a guidebook of consciously earned wisdom for how to walk through such dark struggles and not lose our way. Through the long years of discord with those in the Vatican, the sisters maintained their purpose, sanity, and faith, and created a stronger, more cohesive community of sisters across America and beyond. This treacherous path was continually illuminated by their deepening faith and their skilled processes for collective discernment. They responded thoughtfully and patiently as a community of the faithful discovering ever deeper meaning and solidarity from their trials.

This book makes clear the trials we all encounter as we strive to remain true to our faith in the face of great challenge. It is witness to the power of communal discernment and dialogue. It is testimony to what is possible when authoritarianism is subdued by the compassionate exercise of strength. It is testimony to how we find confidence and clarity in the darkness that leads us forward into the bright, enduring meaning of our work.
-- *Margaret Wheatley, Author*

HOWEVER LONG THE NIGHT: MAKING MEANING IN A TIME OF CRISIS

A SPIRITUAL JOURNEY OF THE LEADERSHIP CONFERENCE OF WOMEN RELIGIOUS (LCWR)

Editor: Annmarie Sanders, IHM

For information about this book or to learn more about the Leadership Conference of
Women Religious, check our website at www.lcwr.org.

ISBN-13: 978-1984984449

Other books by the Leadership Conference of Women Religious:
- *Spiritual Leadership for Challenging Times: Presidential Addresses of the Leadership
  Conference of Women Religious* (Orbis Books, 2014)
- *Transformational Leadership: Conversations with the Leadership Conference of Women
  Religious* (Orbis Books, 2015)

Dedication

To Pope Francis, our brother and friend,
and for all women religious in the world
who share our quest for God

Hard Labor

No C-section for this birth.
You will choose the riskier way,
the way of pushes, gentle or grueling,
of breathing in rhythm with pain.
You choose the wisest midwives,
doulas with muscled hands for you to grip.
They will rub fragrant lotion on pressure points
and murmur into your worst contractions,
"You're doing just fine."

You choose not to dull the pain
but to lean into it.
You labor, long and hard.
Somehow you know that waiting
is labor's hardest part.

-- Regina Bechtle, SC

Table of Contents

Acknowledgements

However Long the Night: Making Meaning in a Time of Crisis was born from long periods of individual and collective discernment about how to share what we learned during a very difficult period for an organization about which we care deeply, the Leadership Conference of Women Religious (LCWR). We, the authors of this book, begin our thanks by acknowledging all who journeyed with us in this discernment – those who helped each of us ponder what we had experienced, sort out our questions, search for wisdom, and then decide if we would share our experience publicly.

Although we were each engaged in our own personal discernment with this question, we knew we also needed to come together to listen to one another and engage in the significant conversations this discernment required. Because we reside in areas all over the United States and beyond, we could not have gathered together without the generous funding we received from the Sisters of St. Joseph of Concordia, Kansas; the Sisters of St. Joseph of Boston; the SC Ministry Foundation; and the Sisters of Charity Foundation of Cleveland. We thank each of these communities and organizations for believing in the necessity and value of communal discernment. With that funding, we were also able to have Cathy Bertrand, SSND guide one of those periods of discernment, and we thank her for such skillful facilitation.

Once we decided to write this book and delved into our individual chapters, we turned to trusted guides and friends to read our chapters and give feedback along the way. We thank each of them, and particularly thank those who read the completed work and provided excellent suggestions for improvement as well as much-appreciated encouragement. These include J Lora Dambroski, OSF; Sharon Euart, RSM; Anne Munley, IHM; Liz Sweeney, SSJ; Marissa Thomas; and Betty Thompson. The expertise each of these women brought to this work made their feedback invaluable. We know that the book is stronger because of them. J Lora's input was especially important since as a former LCWR president, she was involved in the experience we chronicle in this book at its very beginning.

We express our gratitude as well to two other key figures in this journey – Jane Burke, SSND, a former executive director of LCWR, and Mary Whited, CPPS, a former president of the organization. Both were involved in the beginning of the experience and helped shape the way LCWR responded to its crisis. Both also passed away a short time later and thus did not see the situation resolved – at least not from this side of the veil.

There were numerous people with whom LCWR consulted during its six-year journey – theologians, canonists, conflict resolution specialists, philosophers, public relations professionals, and other wise thinkers. The input and ideas from each person considerably influenced how LCWR made this journey, and what we learned throughout the process.

We are grateful as well to the bishops who were appointed as delegates from the Vatican's Congregation for the Doctrine of the Faith to work through this complex situation with LCWR. These men, as well as others from the Vatican who worked with them, were unfailingly respectful and courteous as they labored to understand our experiences and perspectives and enter into true dialogue with us.

Finally, we thank all the Catholic sister leaders who were members of LCWR from 2009-2015, the years when the organization was working through this difficult situation. These women showed enormous resilience and fortitude over those long years when the organization they loved and cherished was in peril. As you will read, the entire LCWR membership engaged in communal discernment throughout those six years, and their insights continually shaped and guided the many decisions that needed to be made. We could not have led the conference as we did without the inner strength of its members, and are humbled by the trust that they placed in us. In addition, we thank the members of the LCWR national office staff, all the thousands of Catholic sisters in the United States and throughout the world, as well as members of the public who supported us all along the way with love, encouragement, and unceasing prayer.

We hope that our deep gratitude to all of you is evident in the words that follow in this book. This collection of what LCWR learned through this six-year experience is as much yours as it is ours.

Marcia Allen, CSJ; Florence Deacon, OSF; Pat Farrell, OSF; Sharon Holland, IHM; Mary Hughes, OP; Janet Mock, CSJ; Annmarie Sanders, IHM; Joan Marie Steadman, CSC; Marlene Weisenbeck, FSPA; Carol Zinn, SSJ

Introduction
What You Will Find in This Book

This book shares our experiences and our learnings as we led the Leadership Conference of Women Religious (LCWR) through a six-year crisis in 2009-2015. You will hear our individual voices as you read the insights that together we have gleaned from our experiences, including values, attitudes, and practices that helped us navigate that time personally and in leading a large national organization. And you will learn how we made very difficult decisions – in community -- using a variety of processes and conceptual frameworks that can be valuable for anyone living or leading in a complex and challenging situation.

Chapter 1 tells the story of why this book came to be and provides background and context for all that follows. *Janet Mock, CSJ* and *Annmarie Sanders, IHM* describe the crisis created for LCWR by the Vatican's doctrinal assessment and mandate, and offer a glimpse of why this crisis was not only personal for many sisters but also, very importantly, a crisis for the organization that represents approximately 80 percent of Catholic women religious in the United States, and a crisis for many US Catholic lay women and men.

Chapter 2 explores truth, conscience, and faithfulness in the context of leadership decisions. These were foundations on which we sought to build our processes and our choices as an organization. *Marlene Weisenbeck, FSPA* conveys the "transformative tension given by God" in our situation, and the importance of attending to conscience in our relationship with God and the teachings of the church. She also offers a methodology for ethical decision-making that can be widely used, and applies it retrospectively to express many factors LCWR considered in its discernment during that time.

Chapter 3 introduces the dispositions and practices that grounded LCWR's deliberations as well as its internal and external communications, enabling thousands of people nationwide to move forward together in a time of great uncertainty. *Pat Farrell, OSF* describes pivotal early experiences to illustrate how we used communal discernment in practice on a very large scale as well as in the deliberations of the board, an approach that powerfully transformed individuals, situations, and the organization as a whole.

Chapter 4 shares the challenges of building right relationships in situations where misunderstanding and distrust have grown over time – so relevant to our current national situation. Questions of truth arise again here. *Janet Mock, CSJ* offers four simple and profound rules for engaging with others in ways that can build genuine dialogue, and describes both the challenges and fruits of our efforts to integrate this approach into our relationships after the issuance of the mandate.

Chapter 5 focuses on the essential work of defining operational values for an organization in crisis. *Marcia Allen, CSJ* and *Florence Deacon, OSF* tell the story of our efforts to align truth, communal discernment, and right relationships in a transformational journey guided by firm principles of nonviolence, dialogue, and personal and communal integrity.

Chapter 6 makes explicit the fact that a transformational journey for an organization is a long, slow series of complex actions, difficult choices, and constant changes that demands the best of the organization's strengths. *Pat Farrell, OSF* looks at LCWR's story with clarity about the specific strengths that we brought to the experience, the fruits of decades of deliberate practices.

Chapter 7 flows from the realization that an undesired journey can open new paths and an organization caught in a very visible, very volatile controversy can discover opportunities to act for a greater public good, beyond the wellbeing of the organization itself. *Carol Zinn, SSJ* tells of LCWR's strong awareness of those who looked to LCWR for some signal or hope, and of our choices to exercise what influence we had to demonstrate that something new could happen in a situation of impasse that felt familiar to many thousands of people other than women religious.

Chapter 8 explores the fact that the roots of "sudden" public conflict had probably been growing strong for many years, in invisible habits of untested perceptions and cultural gaps that can evolve into polarization. *Sharon Holland, IHM* explores the Vatican's confrontation with LCWR from this perspective – both the roots of the conflict and its resolution through growing mutual understanding.

Chapter 9 acknowledges that leadership during a crisis is draining and demanding for the leaders themselves. *Mary Hughes, OP* recounts personal and collective ways in which LCWR leaders found the capacity for personal growth and renewal during this six-year ordeal. In telling these stories, she sheds light on nuances of LCWR's story during those six years.

Chapter 10 brings us face to face with the media, eager for news even when the organization has none to share, eager to tell the contentious story it perceives regardless of a quieter story that may be unfolding behind the scenes. *Annmarie Sanders, IHM* clarifies the questions that an organization must ask itself to determine how, when, and what to communicate to the public; four temptations that may undermine the chosen approach; and personal strategies that can ground public communicators even in the midst of microphones.

Chapter 11 offers a perspective from people who are not part of LCWR. *Solidarity with Sisters* is a group of lay women and men who have been companions to the national office staff since 2012. They share what they have seen and heard, what they learned, and how they apply it to their lives.

You will notice that some experiences and learnings appear in several chapters. It would be impossible for us to offer our personal stories without that overlap. Each of us wrote from our own perspective, influenced by our communal sharing but also particular to our different roles in specific events and our varied professional histories. We hope that the chapters are similar to a musical composition with many unique elements as well as repeated themes that cumulatively convey a richer awareness of important aspects of the whole.

Within the chapters you will also see what it's like to be a sister – or woman religious -- in active ministry in the United States. Our stories are inseparable from our life in faith and in community.

The author biographies give a quick glimpse of our varied experiences. Collectively we have served in a very wide range of church ministries and leadership roles. Among us are educators, canon lawyers, a former staff member at the Vatican, administrators, spiritual directors, consultants, facilitators, and a therapist, all of whom have served on numerous boards of directors in healthcare, education, and other fields. Obviously, we have also been leaders of LCWR. This book will let you see some of LCWR's roles in valued support for hundreds of leaders and tens of thousands of women religious. The author biographies also introduce three members of Solidarity with Sisters, a group with helpful perspective on LCWR's experience from the issuance of the mandate through the present.

The four appendices provide pivotal documents for easy reference.

The glossary is where you can look up unfamiliar words. We have sought to use plain English, but sometimes the official language of the church turned out to be essential. We hope this addition will make this book flow more easily for general readers.

... you will learn how we made very difficult decisions
– in community -- using a variety of processes and
conceptual frameworks that can be valuable for anyone
living or leading in a complex and challenging situation.

1

A Word of Hope to a World in Turmoil

Janet Mock, CSJ and Annmarie Sanders, IHM

This is the story of what was learned by a large national organization, the Leadership Conference of Women Religious (LCWR), during a six-year crisis (2009-2015). A high-ranking and very powerful Vatican office suddenly and very publicly confronted us with forceful questions and negative assumptions about the foundation of our lives as Catholic sisters. The conflict grew more intense midway through those years. The Vatican office threatened the autonomy and even the existence of our organization, an organization on which the great majority of US women religious rely for many kinds of resources, supports, and connections. The experience rocked LCWR's officers, its hundreds of members, and the approximately 60,000 women religious who belonged to member congregations at that time. Yet the ultimate resolution benefitted everyone. How did that happen?

To answer that question, we offer you this book. We believe it will not only explain how we worked through a very difficult situation, but it will provide spiritual grounding, useful information, and perhaps some inspiration and hope to anyone working through a situation of conflict, polarization, or even impasse in their own personal, professional, family, community, neighborhood, or organizational settings.

During this time of heated conflicts and turbulent discord in our nation, we want to describe what we learned about how an organization can navigate past confrontation and impasse to a mutually beneficial resolution. We believe it may be valuable to share our experience and learnings now to describe some of the ways we approached the situation and dealt with challenges. It is important to recognize that this is not only the story of LCWR. The outcome may well have been very different without others who acted with open minds, hearts, and wills so that together we could welcome the action of the Spirit of God in and among us.

The crisis hit us and our organization when the Vatican's Congregation for the Doctrine of the Faith (CDF) shocked LCWR with its 2009 announcement that it was beginning a "doctrinal assessment" – an investigation of LCWR's faithfulness to the church to which women religious have dedicated their lives. We were stunned as well when CDF announced in 2012 that it had concluded its study and was appointing an archbishop who would be assisted by two other bishops to oversee a reform of LCWR as a result of its investigation. (The CDF plan to implement the reform was called the mandate, and is referred to by this term throughout this book. See Appendix A.)

LCWR's identity, autonomy, and survival were in question. LCWR's members – representing approximately 80 percent of the Catholic sisters in the United States – were devastated. No one involved with the situation could see a clear or obvious path toward resolution. The media and the general public (particularly Catholics) gave the situation considerable sustained attention for many reasons, including polarized opinions within the church about what was true and what was false or misunderstood.

During those years and since that time we have been asked by many to tell the story of how the organization and how we as individuals navigated this time of tremendous obvious risk as well as less visible personal pain and, ultimately, blessing. Many reporters and individuals have wanted us to offer an exposé of the unrevealed details of what provoked this investigation and of "who said what when" in the very slow process of its resolution. This is not that tell-all book. This is our serious effort to describe what we learned personally and as an organization about how to weather a crisis in ways that create a new and better reality.

This book is the product of reflection over time. We had long pondered if there was any benefit to our telling LCWR's story and our own stories to the public. We met in December 2015 to debrief together what we had lived as LCWR's leaders at each stage of the process, and to discern whether our story had merit for the wider world. No clear direction came forth from that conversation. The group re-gathered in December 2016 to take up the question again. Our reticence to go public with our stories was palpable primarily because it had been such a sacred journey for us and we wanted it to be respected as such.

However, while meeting in 2016, we were highly conscious of the dire situations in the world -- internationally and nationally. The realities of polarization, dangerous conflicts, and widening cultural chasms were evident in the very air we breathed. As we named the learnings we wanted to remember from our work with this investigation, we began to see more and more clearly their intimate connection to the stark needs present throughout the world.

We began wondering then – could what we had learned from our experience be of service to others? We started listing our insights about what had helped us work through a serious situation that had been built on a series of unaddressed inaccuracies and misinterpretations that spanned decades. We recognized that we had learned a great deal as we and the CDF representatives sorted out differences in ways that were respectful and effective. We recognized as well that what we had learned very likely would benefit others, particularly during these challenging times.

This is our serious effort to describe what we learned personally and as an organization about how to weather a crisis in ways that create a new and better reality.

Our ways of leading LCWR as an organization are not common in the church, in political operations, nor in corporate and non-profit enterprises. LCWR has developed them during more than six decades of continual renewal as we have followed directives from the Second Vatican Council and later church documents. Although our ways of leadership were different, we had to deal with the same challenges that confront any leaders in crises – what goals to pursue, what overall strategies to use, when to share or withhold information within the organization and with the public, what was non-negotiable, how to find or create a solution. As women religious, we called on rich spiritual and cultural traditions. You will glimpse those in this book. We also describe a variety of formal methods, processes, and practices that can readily translate for use in other communities and organizations, large and small. We share our learnings for your consideration as practical options that may help you to create new and better realities in your own parts of the world.

The Leadership Conference of Women Religious

*T*o better understand our experience, some information about the Leadership Conference of Women Religious may be helpful.

LCWR is a member organization for those who lead communities of Catholic sisters throughout the United States. As of this writing, it has more than 1300 members, all Catholic sisters (more often referred to in this book as women religious) who are serving as the leaders of approximately 300 communities of sisters. In total, these leaders represent more than 38,000 women religious in the United States.

The purpose of the organization is to provide education, resources, and networking opportunities for its members. The organization also gives high priority to using its collective voice to advocate for social change and for justice considering the many oppressive and unjust situations plaguing the world and nation.

The organization began in the 1950s at the initiative of the Vatican which sought to bring together the heads of religious orders in national organizations all over the world. This movement started in 1950 when Pope Pius XII convoked an international gathering of the heads of religious orders and told them that their organized collaboration could make them a powerful instrument for the transformation of society. Updating and renewal, however, were needed first. The first National Congress of Religious of the USA was held in 1952, but it took another four years before the heads of women's orders voted to form a national conference. Despite some ambivalence about a need for a conference, the 235 leaders gathered in Chicago unanimously voted on November 24, 1956 to establish what they named the Conference of Major Superiors of Women of the USA (CMSW), later renamed the Leadership Conference of Women Religious.

The historical evolution of LCWR over the next several decades is well-documented in the book, *The Transformation of American Catholic Sisters*,[1] written by Lora Ann Quiñonez, CDP and Mary Daniel Turner, SNDdeN. There the authors, both former executive directors of LCWR, chronicle how the radical transformation of life in the United States between 1960 and 1980 significantly impacted the lives of Catholic sisters. The Second Vatican Council had challenged sisters to return to the stories of the founders of their orders and to do what the founders would do in light of the current needs surrounding them. Many sisters at that time left their traditional ministries of teaching and nursing, in order to serve in the places of greatest need. The book shows how these changes in ministry paralleled gradual changes occurring in the life and spirituality of women religious, as well as in their understandings of the nature of religious life and its purpose.

Noted as well in the book is how these changes also resulted in some conflict with Vatican authorities. While the change taking shape for women religious before Vatican II had been mandated by the church leadership, by the 1970s, the Vatican authorities no longer seemed as positive about renewal, either among women religious or within the church in general. Over the decades, some of the church hierarchy noted their dissatisfaction with sisters reidentifying religious life, speaking out on national issues, and undertaking ministries that were apart from their own communities' sponsored institutions. Central to this tension was disagreement about religious life and its relationship to church authority.

LCWR is governed by a three-person presidency made up of LCWR members who are full-time leaders of their own religious institutes. At its annual assembly, the members of LCWR elect from among their ranks one member who will serve for three years – the first as president-elect, the second as president, and third as immediate past-president. The presidency works in collaboration with a national board, and with the organization's executive director, who is a full-time employee of LCWR. Typically, the three presidents and the executive director are the persons who represent LCWR in meetings with Catholic Church officials.

The Doctrinal Assessment

The governance structure of the Catholic Church is often described as the last true monarchy on earth. The pope is the head of the Catholic Church with ultimate decision-making power exercised for the good of the whole. He is assisted in the administration of the church by offices within the Vatican called the Curia. The Curia oversees matters of state, finances, works of justice and mercy, pastoral concerns, the role of laity, men and women religious, as well as matters related to the church in the modern world. One of these offices within the Curia is the Congregation for the Doctrine of the Faith. Its duty is to protect the patrimony of church doctrine, the deposit of faith that defines the church as Catholic. It is the prerogative of CDF to investigate theologians or institutions that bear the name Catholic to assure orthodoxy within its mission and actions flowing from that mission.

Since LCWR is a public juridic person, that is, an organization with rights and responsibilities protected by canon law, the approved law of the Catholic Church, this organization has a special relationship with the offices within the Curia, especially those having to do with its mission. The three-person presidency and the executive director of LCWR make annual visits to various offices within the Curia to share information about the organization's work and to have conversation with curial personnel about trends worldwide. One of the offices that LCWR visits on a regular basis is the Congregation for the Doctrine of the Faith.

It is the prerogative of CDF to investigate theologians or institutions that bear the name Catholic to assure orthodoxy within its mission and actions flowing from that mission.

At the annual visit of LCWR to CDF in 2001, questions were raised about some of LCWR's speakers and public stances. The LCWR officers answered questions that were asked and the matters seemed to them to have been put to rest. In retrospect, however, it was clear that LCWR remained under suspicion throughout the ensuing decade. On March 9, 2009, the president of LCWR received a letter from the prefect or head of CDF announcing a decision to conduct a doctrinal assessment of the activities and initiatives of LCWR. The letter expressed concern with "both the tenor and doctrinal content of various addresses given at annual assemblies of LCWR," specifically regarding "controverted issues such as the Apostolic letter, *Ordinatio Sacerdotalis,* the Declaration of (CDF's) *Dominus Jesus,* and the problem of homosexuality." The letter went on to explain that the assessment would have as its principal purpose "to review the work of the LCWR in supporting its membership as communities of faith and witness to Christ in today's Church, and to offer any useful assistance." The CDF prefect designated a US bishop to conduct the assessment.

Correspondence from the bishop delegate indicated his concern that "at annual LCWR Assemblies from 2003-2008, some of the guest speakers, officers, and honorees espouse erroneous theological positions and manifest the strong influences of disturbing theological trends, including a general antipathy to the 'institutional church.'" The bishop delegate and the LCWR officers met in person to discuss these concerns, but they reached no resolution. Following the meeting, the bishop sent three questions for LCWR to answer regarding its stance on its relationship with the church and its doctrine. After serious discussion of these questions among the officers, and later with its national board, responses were sent to the bishop. The bishop wrote back several months later to say that CDF wanted the assessment of LCWR expanded to include its programs and resources. He requested that LCWR send to him copies of all its publications, prayer services, descriptions of programs, lists of speakers, assembly content, and resolutions from the previous five years. In March 2010 LCWR sent all the requested materials not only to the bishop, but also to the CDF prefect and the apostolic nuncio to the United States.

In July 2010, the LCWR president received a letter from the bishop delegate stating that all the material he had received from LCWR had been forwarded to CDF and that his work with the assessment was considered as completed.

Unsure if the bishop's letter was an indication that the concerns of CDF had been laid to rest, on April 11, 2011, during the annual visit to CDF, the LCWR officers asked the CDF staff with whom they were meeting if there was any other concern to be addressed. The response was that there were no new concerns.

In preparation for its annual meeting with CDF the following year, LCWR's president received a letter from the prefect of CDF dated February 29, 2012 stating that "it is time to address the conclusions and implementation of the doctrinal Assessment." Because there had been no further conversation about the material that was sent by LCWR to CDF, the officers assumed that what was sent was sufficient response to the questions raised during the assessment. That assumption proved to be unfounded. During the scheduled April 18, 2012 meeting at CDF with LCWR, the officers of LCWR were presented with a mandate of reform of the organization.

The doctrinal assessment from 2009 to 2012 was carried out largely through written communication, telephone calls, and one group meeting with the bishop delegate and the officers of LCWR and a consultant. The mandate itself was carried out by an archbishop delegate and assisting bishop delegates through periodic meetings, usually coinciding with already planned LCWR meetings in different parts of the United States, and through telephone calls. The archbishop delegate attended the annual LCWR national assemblies in 2013 and 2014 and a portion of the LCWR board meetings that followed the assemblies. The three bishop delegates met with LCWR officers twice during the oversight of LCWR by CDF. During these meetings numerous matters were discussed regarding LCWR and its understanding of its role within the church. We believe that these conversations throughout the three years of the implementation of the CDF mandate were essential in forming a working relationship that helped bring the matter to a peaceful close.

The chapters that follow reflect the experience and learnings of the women in leadership in LCWR during the period of the doctrinal assessment, the mandate that followed, and its resolution in 2015. They reflect as well the experience of a group of lay women and men who stood with LCWR in those final three years and since then. Together, we offer you this volume as a word of hope as the world community struggles to understand differences in culture, in perspectives, in codes of ethics, in human values.

In writing this book together, we realize that it was the grace of God and the communion among us that made the journey possible. We offer it to you, the reader, in the hope that you find companions on the journey who help you make meaning and call you to be your best self through the travails of life, as this group did for one another.

Endnotes

1   Lora Ann Quiñonez, CDP and Mary Daniel Turner, SNDdeN, *The Transformation of American Catholic Sisters*. Temple University Press, Philadelphia, 1992.

Together, we offer you this volume as a word of hope as the world community struggles to understand differences in culture, in perspectives, in codes of ethics, in human values.

2

Truth-Telling: On Personal and Institutional Integrity

Marlene Weisenbeck, FSPA

Rise Up Rooted Like Trees

How surely gravity's law,
strong as an ocean current,
takes hold of even the smallest thing
and pulls it toward the heart of the world.
Each thing—
each stone, blossom, child—
is held in place.
Only we, in our arrogance,
push out beyond what we each belong to
for some empty freedom.
If we surrendered
to earth's intelligence
we could rise up rooted, like trees.

Instead we entangle ourselves
in knots of our own making
and struggle, lonely and confused.

So, like children, we begin again
to learn from the things,
because they are in God's heart;
they have never left [God].

This is what the things can teach us:
to fall,
patiently to trust our heaviness.
Even a bird has to do that
before he can fly.
-- Rainer Maria Rilke[1]

PART I -- Introduction[2]

*T*his chapter examines the initial response to the doctrinal assessment as it was communicated on February 20, 2009 as well as the subsequent and more formal document known as the Doctrinal Assessment of the Leadership Conference of Women Religious (referred to as the "mandate") issued on April 18, 2012 which outlined in more specific detail the expectations and work of the assessment (see Appendix A). Specifically, this contribution is intended to convey how truth must be discovered by faithfully attending to one's conscience and its movements toward authentic truth. It will review the church's teaching about fidelity to conscience and offer a view of how discernment can be augmented through one particular method of ethical decision-making.

Reflecting on the ongoing and culminating events of the Vatican doctrinal assessment of the Leadership Conference of Women Religious (LCWR), we could have identified with the story about Jacob journeying to a new place, his unexpected confrontation with an angel (or was it God?), and the persistent wrestling that eventually resulted in Jacob's dislocated hip. Even the angel found the encounter nearly unfathomable and begged to be released by Jacob. But Jacob was not about to let go without receiving a blessing from this rival.

We know the end of the story. Jacob was compelled to reveal his name and the blessing was granted because, the Scripture story says, "Your name shall no longer be Jacob, but Israel; because you have contended with divine and human beings and have prevailed." (Genesis 32:23-33)

Moving Forward Consciously and Conscientiously

The wrestling between Jacob and the angel is a good metaphor for the search for truth and the impetus to live with integrity. Within each person is a sacred space of knowing that directs our decisions and movements into the future. This can also be true in a corporate sense. Leaders consciously perceive, apprehend, and notice with conscientious thought and observation the meaning of the challenges before them and their impact on the broader church and world in which they have a life. An active conscience guides us through such a spiritual journey with careful, upright, and dedicated reflection about what is true and just. Religious authorities who preach establishment ideology without imagination may offer certitude, but no spiritual journey. A spiritual journey and yearning for God is a mystical quest -- a serious posing of the justice question of right relationships which must be approached with nerve. We may be at risk at times, but an authentic conscience will not deny, become cynical, or assimilate what is not right. In the book of Jeremiah, we learn about living a consciously spiritual journey and prophetic call. In situations of conflict and chaos we are impelled toward a new reality which is rooted in who God is and what God desires for the world. In the process we receive a new world given by God, one not believed possible and one sometimes not preferred or chosen.

We accept this transformative tension given by God, even in the context of a surprise announcement such as the doctrinal assessment. We can embrace the reality because our sense of call is a sense of finding God in the midst of confusion and collapse. That sense of God's presence gives us vitality and passion and energy even though we recognize that the outcome will be clear only in retrospect.

Embracing a potentially transformative event inevitably leads to questions about conscience and its role in our lives.

Respected theologians and the Second Vatican Council affirm that attentiveness to conscience is necessary in difficult situations. It was an essential guiding light as LCWR grappled with the reality of the doctrinal assessment.

Bernard Häring, CSsR asserts that conscience is the person's moral authority, the inner core and sanctuary where one knows oneself in confrontation with God and others. In his scholarly discussion about the relationship of conscience and discipleship,[3] he reminds us that the word "conscience" comes from two Latin derivatives: "*cum*" meaning "together," and "*scire*" or "*scientia*" meaning "to know." Our conscience is formed in us through the Word that has called us into being and now calls us to be with the Word in discipleship. Our truest self is inescapably linked with Christ. The Word speaks through our inner voice. We find our name by listening and responding to the One who calls us by name. Häring noted that our conscience is like a candle without a flame. It receives its truth through Christ who is Truth and Light. In a corporate or communal context, Christ the Word of God, is the focal point for sharing experience and reflection in a reciprocity of consciences which are free for each other to give and receive knowledge.

Cardinal Avery Dulles, SJ in reflecting on the role of conscience, stated that conscience is the ultimate subjective norm of all human action. It is not based on a blind feeling or instinct, but a personal considered judgment about what one ought, or ought not, to do or have done. It is never autonomous. There is an obligation to seek guidance and instruction from experts, but we always remain morally free to disregard the experts and go against their recommendations, if we judge that they have erred.[4] Even in the difficult matters in which the teaching office of the church requires "submission of intellect and will,"[5] Dulles states that we cannot make any general statement about what "religious submission of intellect and will" means precisely. Basically, it means that we must give a "respectful readiness to accept" a teaching. Normally, this means something more than a respectful hearing and less than a full commitment of faith.

St. Thomas Aquinas was so convinced about the necessity of acting upon one's conscience that he insisted that one must follow one's conscience, even if it errs. He debated Peter Lombard on this matter, stating that we ought to die excommunicated rather than violate our conscience.[6]

Moving Forward Decisively

The Second Vatican Council made several statements about the role of conscience in the life of Christians. We are reminded in particular of *Dignitatis Humanae* 3 §2[7] and *Gaudium et spes* 16[8] which provide a clear and decisive framework for acting according to our conscience as we search for truth in a manner appropriate to the dignity and social nature of the human person. Such decisive truth-finding is intimately linked to the freedom of faith. To deny these declarations would be to dissent from church teaching.

Within a decade of the close of Vatican II the bishops' conferences in Germany, the United States, and Canada[9] issued pastoral letters giving guidance on the legitimate norms of dissent. With these letters of the three bishops' conferences, it seems impossible to deny that dissent from the non-infallible Magisterium is sometimes licit. To deny this would be to dissent from the teaching of these documents. Dulles, however, wisely advises that the general conditions for dissent are that it should be limited, respectful, and reluctant.

Having carefully reviewed and reflected on the church teachings about conscience, the LCWR officers found it particularly ominous when, during their 2010 meeting with the prefect of CDF, in a discussion about healthcare reform in the United States, we were told to always do what the bishops say even though we have a canonical and civil right to decide differently. The presidency had shown support for healthcare reform by signing a letter of advocacy for the passage of the Affordable Care Act. This was highly controversial because the US bishops opposed the bill, believing that there was no significant evidence that the bill would prohibit funding for abortions. We explained our position which was based on our analysis of the bill and a sincere effort to exercise our affirmation in accord with conscience as well as our rights as citizens. We were given a nod of recognition for this rationale, but the cardinal also noted that while "we are citizens of the earth

> The doctrinal assessment of LCWR inevitably led sisters to a faithful study about conscience and the parameters of dissent.

we are also citizens of a heavenly court. The bishops' opinion should have priority because of their official role as teachers of the faith." We replied that the bishops had not spoken as a conference on the healthcare legislation, and therefore, in light of *Apostolus suos*,[10] which clearly indicates when a teaching is magisterial, the bishops' opinion on healthcare legislation did not fall into the sphere of an official teaching of the church. There was no indication at this meeting that one had a right to exercise one's conscience or that one could have a legitimate dissenting opinion from the bishops. Moreover, we were informed that the doctrinal assessment was an invitation to obedience and deeper living of our vowed life of obedience.[11]

Moving Forward Faithfully

The doctrinal assessment of LCWR inevitably led sisters to a faithful study about conscience and the parameters of dissent. Fidelity to conscience was courageously witnessed by LCWR president Mary Whited, CPPS in 2010 when questioned by a prefect of the Vatican dicastery overseeing religious life: "What shall I tell the pope about you when I visit with him soon?" And Mary responded firmly, "Tell him that we are faithful!"

Collectively, a similar action was declared at the 2012 LCWR assembly following a spirit-filled discernment about how to respond to the doctrinal assessment. Those who attended this assembly would agree that the process and discernment were very much aligned with Bernard Häring's conditions for creative judgment about acting upon conscience. These six conditions include:

1. Yearning for wholeness and openness;
2. Firmness and clarity confirming the natural yearning for those qualities which can be honored as the harvest of the Spirit;
3. Dispositions toward vigilance and prudence;
4. Mutuality of consciences in a milieu where creative freedom and fidelity are embodied with grateful dedication;
5. An actual fidelity, creativity, and generosity in the search for truth in readiness to "act on the Word," and
6. Growth into a new dimension of the good, toward ever fuller light.

Where these conditions still lacked fulfillment, we moved ever securely toward the light that we continuously seek.

LCWR members confirm that when we find ourselves in positions that may differ from what we are told to do or from beliefs of those in roles of authority we live in the tension with arises out of a true love of the church -- the people of God -- and a personal or corporate grounding in faith. Such positions are formed from deep thought, informed consciences, and a profound reverence for human persons. While declaring this, we know that we live our vocations in the heart of the Paschal Mystery which relentlessly calls us to metanoia and the acknowledgement that the church itself is *semper reformanda*, always renewing and reforming itself in order to be more fully identified with Christ and the Gospels.

How do we do this? In authentic faith and praxis, some of the ways that we might attend to our own current experience of renewing our consecrated lives are:

- By developing gestures of mutual blessing,
- By radiating the vigilance of divine love in our commitment to advocate for those with no voice,
- By seeking to engage mutually with the hierarchy in actions that further the mission of Christ and give visible witness to communion in the church,
- By daring to be self-critical of our own actions when others perceive us to be in error,
- By studying in a faithful manner the significance of conscience and the role of legitimate dissent,
- By helping others understand the importance of an informed conscience and the means of forming one's conscience,
- By dredging out the fissures of our hearts where unrecognized misplaced pride wants to be protected,

- By engaging in '*conversatio*' -- an honest exchange of opinion of truth that arises out of silence, reflection, and prayer,
- By continuing a forthright and prophetic call to renewal and reform, understanding that the church is always in need of transformation, and
- By practicing our obedience as an act of intelligent dialogue rather than a sheer submission of will, as an act of learning which draws us nearer to the truth, as a careful listening and discerning within a mutual pursuit of the long-range goal of consensus rather than the short-range goal of order, as a process of sharing different minds and lives and visions in the Body of Christ whose soul is the Holy Spirit.[12]

The church is the living, growing, and dynamic Body of Christ. Through the teachings of Vatican II we have moved from a parochial understanding of our witness to a much broader public witness on behalf of justice and policy. As we continue to examine our congregational stories and founding charisms, we grow in our understanding of who we are rather than being dependent on outside voices to shape our reality. As co-creators with God, our deepest rootedness is in the Spirit. Our message needs to take on even greater urgency and strength especially since so much sincere and respectful feedback to the Magisterium has been dismissed or even ridiculed by some cardinals and bishops.

We will continue to struggle with God and humans, affirming both our brokenness and goodness, and like Jacob and the angel, nurture our gratitude and savor the blessing of the spiritual journey unfolding in every opportune moment for renewal.

> *Jacob crossed over into the Promised Land limping. With the rising sun hitting his face and the smell of morning he had become Israel, a God-wrestler. We are all God wrestlers…. "Lord, we will not let go until you bless us." In the wrestling, we find that God waits for us and that as we cross the river we are not alone. In the wrestling lies a homecoming of the deepest self, the finding of true names, and the discovery of true community. To be blessed is to be wounded. A blessing from God does not grant super-human strength or perfection, but a wounded hip. Walking into the blessing will most certainly mean suffering as well as hope, brokenness as well as grace. We feel the morning sun on our cheek[s] and are grateful to be limping.[13]*

PART II
A Method for Ethical Decision-Making as Applied to the Experience of the Doctrinal Assessment of LCWR

*U*pon receiving the February 20, 2009 letter from CDF informing us about the doctrinal assessment that was to be conducted, the LCWR presidency immediately began to communicate with the board, the conference as a whole, past presidents of LCWR, canonists and theologians, the apostolic nuncio, the bishop delegate, and other consultants. Intuitively, we approached the situation in ways that relied on our native abilities which were also supported by years of experience in multiple church ministries and leadership practice. We found that it was possible to handle complex ethical and ecclesial problems without relying on sophisticated theories. Indeed, there was no effort to seek out or act upon any particular theory of conflict resolution. Our first response was to enter into a contemplative discernment that would help us set the stage for a respectful and honest dialogue with church authorities. In retrospect, we observed that we actually had mirrored a four-way method for ethical decision-making outlined by professional ethicists.[14] It is framed on a schema with dimensions about truth, consequences, fairness, and character as depicted in the following graphic.

Four-Way Method for Ethical Decision-Making

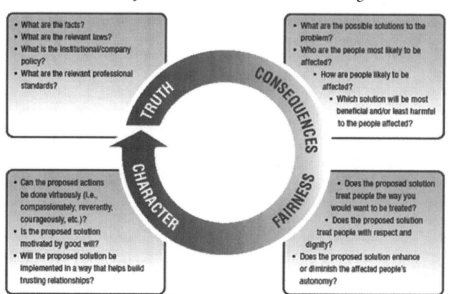

The following examples indicate how our response to the doctrinal assessment was reflected in this methodology for ethical decision-making.

TRUTH

What are the facts?

- The doctrinal assessment was the result of several years of suspicious and clandestine examination of potential doctrinal error that others presumed to be found in LCWR publications and conference activities.
- The LCWR presidency was informed verbally by the prefect of the Congregation for Institutes of Consecrated Life and Societies of Apostolic Life (CICLSAL) that cardinals from the US serving in Rome were requesting an investigation of LCWR. The presidents of LCWR requested a meeting with these cardinals, but the prefect of CICLSAL noted that such a meeting would not be a "peaceful" experience.
- LCWR, *ipso facto*, was removed from oversight by CICLSAL when a team of other bishop delegates was appointed to implement the assessment. LCWR continued, however, to consult with and report to CICLSAL throughout the process.
- The primary concern was the doctrine of faith as revealed by Christ, scripture, and tradition under the official teaching of the Magisterium.
- CDF perceived corporate dissent on the part of "officers" of LCWR which suggested collective dissent by the conference.
- Interpretations of LCWR statements, assembly resolutions, and keynote addresses were read out of context or misquoted. LCWR was concerned about an alternate agenda because of questionable analysis on the part of CDF. A seemingly misunderstood use of the term "radical feminism" created, in the minds of the bishop delegates, and possibly distorted CDF views of LCWR's faith in the saving mission of Jesus Christ, the structures of sacramental life, and the impression of an alternative magisterium.
- Some areas where LCWR was charged with promoting controverted church teaching were never declared to be part of the ordinary and universal magisterial teachings. (*Dominus Jesus*, US bishops' statement on the Affordable Care Act)
- A verbal request was made by the initial bishop delegate for LCWR to sign a statement of disavowal on issues of ordination of women, homosexuality, and other historic resolutions considered doctrinally incorrect and inadequate.
- The goal was the renewal and reform of LCWR to be accomplished through various forms of canonical intervention.
- There was a denial of rights when the CDF prefect insisted LCWR must

"always do what the bishop says" (even though conscience and canon/ civil law indicate otherwise).

- LCWR attempted to maintain integrity and transparency through annual visits and regular reporting to CDF.

What are the relevant laws?

- Canon 708,[15] Canon 709[16] and other canons pertaining to consecrated life as well as the rights of the hierarchy
- Vatican II documents
- *Vita Consecrata* 46 [17]
- *Apostolos suos*
- USCCB Ethical and Religious Directives for Catholic Health Care Services

What is the institutional/company policy?

- It was never the practice nor intent of LCWR to publicly stand in opposition to church teaching on any matter.
- LCWR consistently sought trustworthy advisors in order to act on the principle of nonmaleficence (doing no harm, or minimizing the risk of harm to others).

What are the relevant professional standards?

- Ethical, balanced dialogue based on truth
- Canonical administrative appeal, as a last option

CONSEQUENCES

What are the possible solutions to the problem?[18]

- Authentic mutual dialogue between CDF and LCWR could bring about greater clarity, more informed understanding, and better relationships between these entities.
- The Holy See could constrain LCWR's autonomy as an organization by requiring, for example: confirmation by the Holy See of LCWR's presidential elections, approval by the Holy See of speakers employed by LCWR, or that LCWR offer conferences on certain doctrinal topics.
- A liaison or apostolic delegate with authority for certain decisions could be imposed on LCWR.
- Suppression of the conference, though rare in the case of public juridic persons, would involve consultation with the major governance body. Disposition of assets and goods would be governed by canon and civil law.

- LCWR presidents and board members could be asked to take an oath of fidelity (with "submission of intellect and will").
- Presidents and board members could be asked to sign statements disavowing the statements of certain LCWR assembly keynote addresses.
- Presidents and board members could be removed subsequent to refusal to follow directives of the bishops moderating the implementation of the doctrinal assessment.
- There could be the possibility of doctrinal requirements for membership in LCWR, such as signing a statement of doctrinal fidelity.
- Collaboration with other organizations deemed doctrinally controverted might result in additional investigations of those organizations.
- Attempts to regulate specific prayer forms at official functions of the conference could be imposed.
- The right to engage in theological and spiritual discourse might be threatened.
- LCWR statutes could be revised.

Who are the people most likely to be affected?

- LCWR and its member congregations
- Other conferences of women and men religious around the world were concerned about a precedent being set for their conferences.
- The whole church was likely to be affected by way of the example of how doctrinal matters could be enforced in other spheres of church life and practice.

How are people likely to be affected?

- The perception was that it would be highly negative and explosive for LCWR, women religious, and the wider church.
- Many viewed the CDF process as lacking transparency.

Which solution will be most beneficial and/or least harmful to the people affected?

- One based on mutual recognition of adult behaviors
- One recognizing the necessity of mutual respect
- One sought with equal participation in design of the outcome
- One that was ethical on the part of all
- One that honored and respected the differences held by both parties
- One that demonstrated transparency
- One that demonstrated appropriate interpretation of church law and teaching
- One that upheld the mission and values of LCWR

FAIRNESS

Does the proposed solution treat people the way you want to be treated?
- Imposition of canonical interventions almost always has an odious dimension.
- Integrity in relationships was found to be prerequisite for openness to truth and authentic dialogue.

Does the proposed solution treat people with respect and dignity?
- It was perceived that judgments were made on the faith and life of women religious in member congregations. As an example, a president of LCWR was queried directly on her personal belief in Jesus Christ by a bishop delegate.
- The LCWR's October 20, 2009 written response to CDF was considered "inadequate," but with no explanation provided by CDF.

Does the proposed solution enhance or diminish the affected people's autonomy?
- The bishop delegate's findings submitted to CDF on December 22, 2009 were never shared with the presidency of LCWR.
- Clarifications provided by LCWR of questions concerning LCWR assembly resolutions were apparently ignored.
- The ultimate conclusion of the process by CDF provided a review and renewal of religious life in the United States as well as a potential future model for the requirements of church law pertaining to conferences of major superiors.
- The principle of human dignity and respect for autonomy was upheld in the final outcome as evidenced in the noninterference in the decisions of competent persons and the empowerment of others for whom the conference is responsible.

CHARACTER

Can the proposed actions be done virtuously (i.e., compassionately, reverently, courageously, etc.)?
- The May 27, 2009 meeting with the bishop delegate transpired in a calm way; though cordial, he appeared inadequately prepared or informed about the nature of his task.
- The public processing of pain concerning the events can be important for resolution. Nonetheless, there is a time to speak and a time to be silent, as was the policy of LCWR with the media.

Is the proposed solution motivated by good will?

- The Ordinary Session of CDF on January 12, 2011 decided that this LCWR matter was of sufficient gravity because of the "influence" that this could have in other parts of the world.
- The renewal and reform of LCWR hoped to offer an important contribution to the future of religious life in the United States.
- The overarching concern was to assist LCWR in implementing an ecclesial communion founded on faith in Christ; that is, "to consolidate the unity and communion among the different bodies that make up the wider family of the Church."

Will the proposed solution be implemented in a way that helps build trusting relationships?

- The ultimate solution achieved in 2015 did build more trusting relationships, but not without the principle of beneficence (obligation to bring about good in all our actions) having been bruised in the process.
- The principle of justice was achieved; that is, both parties in the dispute (church authorities and LCWR) received what was owed and deserved with no unfair burdens imposed. LCWR statutes were agreeably revised and a plan for reviewing publications was implemented.

The assumptions and activities noted above indicate some of the principal factors involved in the doctrinal assessment. As the doctrinal assessment transpired, it became more and more evident that CDF was operating out of a hierarchical model of the church where unquestioning obedience to church authority is called for, while at the same time LCWR was acting and living out of the church model conceived as communion where dialogue and consensus would be the norm. The latter thereby supports the idea of corporate conscience where decisions are achieved out of "knowing together" and thus provides more clarity about knowledge of the truth, morally and practically.[19] With different schemas of understanding, the tensions and dilemmas experienced by both entities in bringing the assessment to conclusion were inevitable.

The gestures of CDF stepping into our space and scrutinizing the faith and practice of conference members' activities presented a certain personal and institutional suffering for LCWR. In those actions, we felt reduced to nakedness in the face of those who prescribed how we must stand before them in the process of the assessment. Instead of seeing us as leaders of a conference of women religious who have agency in our own right,[20] the process became a means to an end, a vessel of satisfaction for what was determined to be the goal of the doctrinal assessment. It felt as if we were not viewed as having the capacity to properly serve the mission of LCWR or to engage the ecclesial structures. This was the greatest source of our suffering – having our personal, congregational, and conference identity examined and surely humiliated during various parts of the process. Maybe it was how Christ felt before Pilate. We wondered, would this be our final judgment?

> Without a doubt, our greatest source of grace during this time was coming to know more fully God's absolute and unconditional fidelity to us, our communities, and the whole conference.

Adding to this suffering was how our October 2009 response to CDF was discounted, after having had the structure for the response agreed upon with the prelate in charge. And more poignant still were the deaths of Mary Whited, CPPS (LCWR president, 2006-2009) and Jane Burke, SSND (LCWR executive director, 2008-2011) who served with us during this time. Both died of cancer before this assessment was resolved. We know how deeply they felt about this assessment and how they wept.

Without a doubt, our greatest source of grace during this time was coming to know more fully God's absolute and unconditional fidelity to us, our communities, and the whole conference. We are grateful especially to our community members who could express their appreciation in the ways that they were able and to the laity who have supported the US Catholic sisterhood through all this in remarkably creative and persistent ways.

Truly, we have not been alone in moving forward in what appeared to be a confrontation with church authorities. God has been our stronghold and the church has risen in solidarity. We know the broken hip along with the blessing! Our outward witness of gratitude, joy, hope, and meekness are sure signs of the Holy Spirit's presence with us. In authentic humility, we consciously know the ground of our being and the integrity that would not let go of this struggle until we emerged as a new people, renewed and reconciled in the mystery of paschal love.

Rooted
in sacred space of knowing
bending and bowing to the dispatch
in quiet awe - never swaying to threats of silencing
that would deny us of believing the Word --
ensconced in lives of beatitude love
rooted deeply in the Christ that would light the way
for conversatio leading to knowledge and fortitude
becoming a new people of the Word
rising up like a tree
enfleshed
for
timeless
and
Faithful
Foresight
-- Marlene Weisenbeck, FSPA

For Reflection and Dialogue

1. Have you ever found yourself in a situation where your conscience urged you to respond differently than what authorities recommended as a solution? How did you respond?

2. When have you found yourself in an ethical or legal dilemma where a structured or systematic process for reflection based on truth, consequences, fairness, and character would have enhanced your decision-making process for moving forward?

Endnotes

1. "Wenn etwas mir vom Fenster fallt …/ How surely gravity's law" by Rainer Maria Rilke from Rilke's *Book of Hours* by Rainer Maria Rilke, translated by Anita Barrows and Joanna Macy, translation copyright © 1996 by Anita Barrows and Joanna Macy. Used by permission of Riverhead, an imprint of Penguin Publishing Group, a division of Penguin Random House LLC. All rights reserved.

2. This introduction is substantially borrowed from an article written by Marlene Weisenbeck, FSPA, "Moving Forward Securely, Consciously, Decisively, Faithfully." *LCWR Occasional Papers*, Winter 2013. Used with permission.

3. Bernard Häring, "Conscience: The Sanctuary of Creative Fidelity and Liberty." Chapter 20 in *Introduction to Christian Ethics: A Reader*, eds. R. Hamel & K. Himes, Paulist Press, New York (1989), 252 - 280. This article originally appeared in *Free and Faithful in Christ*, Vol. 1 (New York: Seabury Press, 1978) 223 - 284.

4. Avery Robert Dulles, "Authority and Conscience." *Church* (Fall 1986) 8-15. http://vatican2voice.org/8conscience/dulles.htm

5. *The Code of Canon Law*. Canon 752.

6. *Scriptum super libros Sententiarum*, IV, 38, 2.4 q.a 3; see also IV.27.1.2.q.a.4ad3; Iv.27, 3.3. *expositio*.

7. *Dignitatis Humanae* 3 §2 "The individual must not be forced to act against conscience nor be prevented from acting according to conscience, especially in religious matters. The reason is because the practice of religion of its very nature consists primarily of those voluntary and free internal acts by which human beings direct themselves to God. Acts of this kind cannot be commanded or forbidden by any merely human authority . . ."

8. *Gaudium et spes* 16 "In the depths of his conscience, the human person detects a law which he does not impose on himself but which holds him to obedience. Always summoning him to love good and avoid evil, the voice of conscience can, when necessary, speak to his heart more specifically: do this, shun that. For man has in his heart a law written by God. To obey it is the very dignity of the person; according to it he will be judged (cf. Rom 2:15-16). Conscience is the most secret core and sanctuary of a person. There he is alone with God whose voice re-echoes in his depths. In a wonderful manner conscience reveals that law which is fulfilled by love of God and neighbor (cf. Mt 22:37-40; Gal 5:14). In fidelity to conscience, Christians are joined with the rest of men in search for truth and for the genuine solution to the numerous problems which arise in the life of individuals and from social relationships. Hence, the more a correct conscience holds sway, the more persons and groups turn aside from blind choice and strive to be guided by objective norms of morality."

9. See West German bishops on norms for dissent (1967) and National Conference of [USA] Catholic Bishops *Norms of Licit Theological Dissent* (1968) found in Charles E. Curran and Richard A. McCormick, SJ *Readings in Moral Theology* No. 6, New York: The

Missionary Society of St. Paul the Apostle (1988) 127-132, and Canadian Conference of Catholic Bishops *Statement on the Formation of Conscience* (1 December 1973) at www.consciencelaws.org/issues-ethical/ethical040.html.

10. *"Apostolus suos."* *Acta Apostolicae Sedis* 90 (September 1, 1998, no.7) 640. www.vatican.va/archive/aas/documents/AAS-90-1998-ocr.pdf *"In order that the doctrinal declarations of the Conference of Bishops . . . may constitute authentic magisterium and be published in the name of the Conference itself, they must be unanimously approved by the Bishops who are members, or receive the recognition of the Apostolic See if approved in plenary assembly by at least two-thirds of the Bishops belonging to the Conference and having a deliberative vote. . . No body of the Episcopal Conference, outside the plenary assembly, has the power to carry out acts of authentic magisterium. The Episcopal Conference cannot grant such power to commissions or other bodies set up by it."*

11. This also was Cardinal Levada's final statement in an interview two years later with the *National Catholic Reporter*. John L. Allen, Jr. "Exclusive interview: Levada talks LCWR, criticism in the States." *National Catholic Reporter* (June 15, 2012). www.ncronline.org/blogs/all-things-catholic/exclusive-interview-levada-talks-lcwr-criticism-states

12. Adapted and paraphrased from William Cavanaugh's thoughts on the Catholic tradition of obedience as articulated for the Catholic Common Ground Initiative (2010).

13. Sarah Hennessey. "Circle of Relationships." La Crosse, WI: *FSPA Incorporation News* (Spring 2008) 4-5.

14. Richard Kyte. *An Ethical Life: A Practical Guide to Ethical Reasoning.* Winona, MN: Anselm Academic. 2012. Graphic used with permission.

15. *The Code of Canon Law.* Canon 708: *"Major superiors can be associated usefully in conferences or councils so that by common efforts they work to achieve more fully the purpose of the individual institutes, always without prejudice to their autonomy, character, and proper spirit, or to transact common affairs, or to establish coordination and cooperation with the conference of bishops and also with individual bishops."*

16. Ibid. Canon 709: *"Conferences of major superiors are to have their own statutes approved by the Holy See, by which alone they can be erected even as a juridic person and under whose supreme direction they remain."*

17. *Vita Consecrata* 46 iterated the distinctive aspects of ecclesial communion to include full participation and ready obedience to bishops and the pope, especially by theologians, teachers, publishers, catechists, and means of social communication.

18. These points were made by canonists who advised LCWR when they met with the conference in 2012 and some were part of the CDF "Doctrinal Assessment of the Leadership Conference of Women Religious," published on April 18, 2012. Cardinal Gerhard Müller emphasized some of them in his opening remarks to the LCWR presidents on April 30, 2014.

19. Michael G. Lawler and Todd A. Salzman. "Following Faithfully." *America* (February 2, 2015) 16-19.

20. In philosophy and sociology, agency is the capacity of an agent (a person or other entity, human or any living being in general, or soul-consciousness in religion) to act in any given environment. The capacity to act does not at first imply a specific moral dimension in the ability to make the choice to act, and moral agency is therefore a distinct concept. In sociology, an agent is an individual engaging with the social structure. One's agency is one's independent capability or ability to act on one's will. This ability is affected by the cognitive belief structure which one has formed through one's experiences, and the perceptions held by the society and the individual, of the structures and circumstances of the environment one is in and the position into which one is born.

In authentic humility,
we consciously know the ground of our being and the
integrity that would not let go of this struggle until we
emerged as a new people, renewed and reconciled
in the mystery of paschal love.

3

The Gift and Challenge of Communal Discernment

Pat Farrell, OSF

May you know the wisdom of deep listening,
The healing of wholesome words,
The encouragement of the appreciative gaze,
The decorum of held dignity,
The springtime edge of the bleak question.[1]
-- John O'Donohue

Just four months after the Congregation for the Doctrine of the Faith (CDF) issued a mandate to the Leadership Conference of Women Religious (LCWR), the conference was gathered with unusually large attendance at its 2012 national assembly. As the event was coming to a close, Annmarie Sanders, IHM, LCWR's communications director, stood before the group and read a proposed public position statement, summarizing members' deliberations about how to respond to the mandate. (See Appendix B.) A spontaneous standing ovation and thunderous applause immediately followed the reading, indicating quick and easy approval by the assembly. A certain quiet then fell over the group. There was a palpable sense of gratitude, relief, and awe. In the span of just four days 900 congregational leaders of very divergent positions were able to endorse a common direction at a very critical, emotionally charged moment. Amazing! There was a recognition that we had just participated in a process that included us but that was also beyond us. There had been honest dialogue, a sense of the sacred, and real communal discernment. Many of us went away wondering at how it all came to be.

Among the many relationships LCWR needed to tend with great care during the doctrinal assessment process was the relationship with and among its own members. Public focus at the time looked more to LCWR's relationship with other key players: CDF, bishop delegates, Catholic laity, the United States Conference of Catholic Bishops, the media, the Vatican. Without a doubt, building a relational climate with them which would allow genuine dialogue was of the essence. But LCWR's constituency of elected leaders of US women's congregations was the group most directly affected by the mandate and the body holding the organization's power of decision-making. Good communication among us was essential. Mutual trust was necessary to move forward together. None of us wanted LCWR to be divided as a conference as a result of the CDF mandate, even as we were aware of differences among us in the face of a complex situation.

With hindsight two important elements had been key components of LCWR's effective process in determining a response to the Vatican mandate: contemplative reflection for communal discernment, and participative processes which facilitated inclusivity and mutuality. Let me describe both.

For a year or more prior to receiving the CDF mandate, LCWR had been guiding its members in learning a process of group contemplative reflection (See Appendix D.) It was very timely. The large-scale upheaval of one era fading and another trying to come to birth was more and more evident. Large global shifts were making themselves felt all around us. In that context, it was becoming clear that US women's congregations, facing a very uncertain future, needed to discern a way forward together from a place of spiritual depth. LCWR gatherings at national, regional, and local levels had begun using a contemplative reflection process as a way of hearing together how God was beckoning us forward. The method used was a form of communal discernment, weaving significant time for silent reflection with group sharing from a depth of listening. It was becoming a familiar and much appreciated practice just when the CDF mandate was given to LCWR.

LCWR members also have an experiential fluency with participative processes of self-governance. Many of us believe that an important legacy of US women religious to the church and world is the re-structuring and re-visioning of models of self-directed common life, inspired by the ecclesial document, *Perfectae Caritatis*. In response to the renewal invited by Vatican II, we created participative structures of leadership and of the exercise of authority and obedience. Decision-making became consultative, participative, a collective effort to hear the voice of God's Spirit discerned through and from the whole. These changes, while neither foolproof nor without error, offered some corrective to the authoritarianism which lent itself to domination and the abuse of power. Participative, relational processes for decision-making came to be a taken-for-granted part of who we are. They are operative in congregational structures as well as in the organizational design of LCWR, including in its three-person presidency. Those structures, well in place, were the given framework into which the mandate of the doctrinal assessment was given to US women religious.

> *Decision-making became consultative, participative, a collective effort to hear the voice of God's Spirit discerned through and from the whole.*

These processes formed the backdrop, the set of givens, for how LCWR moved into formulating a response to the CDF mandate. A number of other procedural elements were also enormously helpful. I offer a sampling of them by recounting in detail two key LCWR gatherings: the first national board meeting and the first national assembly after receiving the mandate. LCWR's response unfolded over a three-year period and at each juncture modes of proceeding specific to the circumstances were utilized. However, the two critical LCWR meetings I will describe are illustrative of the general approach and style used throughout.

First Meeting of the LCWR National Board

In preparation for the first national board meeting after receiving the mandate, in May 2012, the presidents and executive director of LCWR communicated with the executive committee of the national board by conference call, recounting their experience in Rome and answering questions. A precedent was established in that call: sharing as much information as possible at suitable levels, and agreeing to appropriate confidentiality in judiciously deciding what information to make public when. That guiding pattern served us well throughout the entire process.

When the board met in person, we benefited from the help of a psychologist who led us in a process to surface and express emotions. The hope was to create a safe environment to communicate feelings openly so that the potential negative impact of anger and sadness would not create a toxic environment or cloud clear discernment of a response. Those feelings needed to be processed in order to harness and direct their energy. There were many emotions in the room, and we wanted to consciously integrate the force of those feelings into an unfolding process. It took time. The catharsis was clearly only a beginning, but helpful and instructive. A deeper bond had been forged among those present. We could see the need for and the value of doing something similar with the broader LCWR membership. At strategic points we did convene extra regional meetings for members to air feelings, provide mutual support, listen to one another, and strategize together in anticipation of critical decisions.

Another support at that first board meeting was the presence of a spiritual director, attending the process, listening for movements of the Spirit and reflecting that to the group at different moments. It was a great help in keeping all of us attentive to the divine presence within and among us. To what was God inviting us at this moment in time? What Scripture spoke to us? How were we being led? The spiritual director intermittently gave feedback and invited silent reflection, prayer, or conversation. Her very presence was a call to live the process of responding to the CDF mandate from an awareness of God's presence and leading. We were invited to deep listening.

Why was the presence of a spiritual director important to us? Our desire was to be led into the most faithful response we could give at a moment when it was not easy to determine, in the heat of the moment, what was of God and what wasn't. It was a great benefit to have an outside ear listening for what might be the source of the responses that were surfacing. Were they coming from anger, from peace, from sincere searching, from an agitated soul, from knee-jerk emotions, from a listening heart? It was also helpful to have someone being consciously attentive to subtle movements of the Spirit in the group while each of us was more intently focused on the business at hand. Only through deep listening for God at work in our deliberations could we feel confident of being capable of moving toward right action.

Our listening included attempts to gather what we were hearing from LCWR members locally. Each board member summarized feedback she was getting from her geographical region. It was important to consider the experiences, concerns, and suggestions the national board members had been hearing from their members and to incorporate that perspective into our discernment.

There was also very deliberate gathering of needed information. Beginning with this first board meeting, and throughout the entire process, LCWR invited the perspective of various consultants. We heard from civil lawyers to better understand the rights and responsibilities of the national board in its role in the civil corporation of LCWR. A canon lawyer shared observations on the CDF document from the viewpoint of canon law, reflecting on its implications for LCWR as an entity with canonical status as a public juridic person. A prominent layman gave suggestions of ways to interface with the laity whose concerns for the church had been newly triggered by the mandate. At other key moments we invited the wisdom of theologians, as well as experts in organizational dynamics, nonviolent conflict transformation, and communications.

This input was intertwined with varied methods of small and large group processing. We asked what seemed to be coalescing, becoming clear. We considered what might be guiding principles, LCWR non-negotiables, in formulating a response to the mandate. We heard each person in turn reflect on possible next steps. We formulated possible scenarios. Perhaps most significantly, we engaged in a lengthy contemplative reflection process, a communal discernment tool now familiar to LCWR members. In that deep listening there seemed to emerge a greater clarity about who we are and who we are called to be, about what really matters and what doesn't. A few of the emerging insights from that discernment:

- We believe in the transformative power of the Holy Spirit. We embrace through grace the greater public role into which we have been thrust.
- LCWR, with our companions in faith, responds to the Spirit's call to speak truth with love and courage.
- We are immersed in larger issues of reform in the church and will be faithful to our role as midwives and participants.
- We are called to not be afraid and to remain interiorly free, regardless of what the exterior looks like. We are called to remain faithful to the Gospel, and to our mission for the future of the church.
- We are at a moment of convergence of lots of energies at the foot of the cross. The convergence is coming in the hope of, and the fear of, new life.

The contemplative reflection process created a greater peace and unity among those present which made easier some of the crucial tasks remaining. A public statement had to be written for release to the large number of reporters awaiting its publication at the close of the meeting. The process was again participative. An initial draft was written by a small group, brought to the large group for feedback, considered in a process guided by the spiritual director, tweaked and approved. The board considered a communications plan for dealing with the media and approved a press release. The group determined to call an extra geographical regional meeting before the August assembly, providing an opportunity for members to air feelings and concerns, to identify non-negotiable values to safeguard, and to consider options before coming together nationally and facing the pressure of critical decisions. The board prepared a guide to follow for that meeting and composed a letter from the national board to the LCWR members, sharing as much information as was appropriate. Knowing that the media coverage of this first board meeting would be extensive, all members were provided talking points in the event they were asked to comment on this matter by their local media outlets.

We came to recognize the grace of not seeing a way out of the challenge we faced.

Important patterns and understandings were established at that first board meeting. We came to recognize the grace of not seeing a way out of the challenge we faced. It was very clear that we had to discern together, that we depended on and needed one another as never before, that we were to entrust ourselves to the larger divine movement which was holding and carrying us. It was evident that we were dealing with something larger than ourselves. We were invited to hold the tensions and to discover unseen ways beyond polarization and dualities. We needed to pray and discern our way through the months ahead with honest dialogue, relationship-building, careful communication, consultation, transparency, anticipation, and thorough planning. We were on our way, not knowing where the path ahead would lead, but headed there together.

First LCWR National Assembly

As LCWR members gathered for the 2012 national assembly in St. Louis, intense public interest was evident in the large number of requests for media credentials and by the crowds gathered in support outside the convention site. In recognition of the sympathetic demonstrators, members present at the assembly were invited to accompany the LCWR presidency as they addressed the crowds and mingled with the supporters.

More delicate was the careful relating to the multitude of media contacts present. There would be no official communication available to the media until the close of the assembly when the presidency was to hold a press conference on the outcome of LCWR's deliberations. The communications strategy for the time prior to that was to take advantage of the moment by providing educational sessions to help the media understand religious life and the context of the doctrinal assessment. Each day different panels of sisters briefed them on background information: how religious life came to be as it is today, the role of contemplation and dialogue, LCWR's history and emerging future.

Communication with LCWR members was, of course, most important. A critical task would be sharing information and carefully listening to the wisdom of the group. Former LCWR presidents were invited to a session with the presidents and executive director before the opening of the assembly. They represented the history of LCWR as it faced other critical moments. The wealth of their insights was invaluable.

The assembly included a closed session to allow members the freedom to muddle towards a gradually emerging direction without precipitous outside interpretation and speculation. In that environment, confidential updates were shared as well as clarifying information concerning implications of directions LCWR might choose. Possible scenarios in response to the CDF mandate were presented, inviting the creativity of the assembly to modify them and to elaborate others. The two facilitators guiding the process had strategized carefully how to enable attentive listening and candid dialogue. Much thought was given to creating conditions for the expression and consideration of minority viewpoints. There would be small- and large-group conversations, time-limited open-mike sharing, randomly selected samplings of group conclusions, and large-group leanings, interspersed with times of contemplative silence. What was slowly distilled in the process was the group sense to proceed in dialogue with the bishop delegates so long as LCWR's mission and integrity would not be compromised. It was not, however, until LCWR members heard their indistinct consensus reflected to them in a well-articulated statement that the recognition of a discerned direction settled peacefully over the group.

Communal Discernment

The 2012 assembly was an experience of communal discernment, and it was a gift. LCWR members convened, initially unable to see a clear way forward. That alone was a starting point of grace, much as it appeared to be anything but that. Our acknowledged unknowing was a fortuitous fertile field for genuine discernment. Out of the urgency of felt need we listened collectively to how God's Spirit was guiding us. Ultimately, we were able to see together with the eyes of our common heart more than any one of us could have seen alone. An African proverb says: "It is because one antelope will blow the dust from the other's eye that the two antelopes will walk together."[2] In our precarious walking and attentive listening to one another, God's transformative presence somehow enabled us to access a pool of wisdom arising from our collective consciousness. We were carried together in a direction which only gradually showed itself and which stretched beyond our own effort.

Though the intensity and drama of this national assembly made it an unprecedented event, the experience sounded a note of familiarity for many of us. In our community lives, women religious have often lived critical moments of tension and struggle in group decision-making. At times we have experienced genuine communal discernment, enabling us to move forward together in harmony. At other times we have been left facing unresolved issues, despite our best efforts. Clearly the outcome does not depend solely on well-designed procedures. Communal discernment is simultaneously what we do and what God does. On our part, there are helpful predispositions we can bring to the process.

> *Staying with ambiguity leaves us open to the unexpected movement of Spirit. It requires trust.*

One is the sort of uncertainty with which we entered the LCWR national assembly. To come with minds made up or with predetermined solutions would present a serious obstacle to group discernment. A necessary predisposition is an open mind, open heart, and open will, laying aside judgment, cynicism, and fear.[3] Staying with ambiguity leaves us open to the unexpected movement of Spirit. It requires trust.

Another helpful disposition is deep listening, to both internal and external voices. Attentiveness to interior movements requires noticing whatever arises in the moment. It also includes being present to our own history and experience, to all that has shaped who we are, to the relationships and values to which we desire to be faithful. LCWR's awareness of that was important in discerning what a response of integrity meant for us. Listening to external voices required open and receptive relationship with bishop delegates, CDF, CICLSAL, concerned Catholic laity, LCWR members, religious throughout the world. We were challenged at every level of dialogue to listen for mutuality within unfamiliar, discordant, variant voices. Commitment to relationship and commitment to deep listening seemed inseparable.

In listening to external voices, Pope Francis describes the need to be grounded in what is concretely before us. He says that discernment "must be embodied in the circumstances of place, time and people. It is always done in the presence of the Lord, looking at the signs, listening to the things that happen, the feeling of the people, especially the poor…. The wisdom of discernment redeems that necessary ambiguity of life and helps us find the most appropriate means, which do not always coincide with what looks great and strong." [4]

Similarly, a commitment to truth is essential to discernment. It implies honest self-awareness, of being with rather than running from the truth of our own experience, including those feelings and attitudes we'd rather not have or those we are slow to recognize and embrace. It demands simply being with what is, rather than what we might prefer. It involves courage and the discipline of honest dialogue and, for that, the willingness to be vulnerable.

Communal discernment presupposes a readiness to be transformed, a willingness to be changed by an encounter with another. It invites us to recognize both the light and the shadow present in who we are together. To recognize our group shadow invites openness to being challenged, purified, molded, questioned. To see our own light leads us to claim our gifts and to put them at the service of the greater whole, to stand boldly in our own truth.

Personal and communal freedom is another important predisposition, implying fearlessness, an indifference to outcomes, and a willingness to assume the consequences of a group direction. The freedom to choose comes in paying attention to what brings peace, to what causes agitation and unsettledness, and moving in the direction of peace.

There is hard work involved. We must do the homework of gathering information, working together to understand, sort through, imagine options, critique, and manage processes. We need to consciously integrate our real feelings. And then we need to simply surrender, to let go of desired results. We even need to let go of the timing. It is not helpful to either rush to decide too quickly, or draw things out unnecessarily, delaying or avoiding difficult decisions. The process takes place in limited, real time, but also needs the spaciousness of its own unfolding.

Finally, discernment is prayer. It is a conscious opening to God's Spirit, inviting transformation. In the LCWR assembly, the prayerful silence integrated into the process was empowering, as was the prayer of so many others directed toward us during that time together.

The 2012 LCWR assembly ended with a decision, with a public statement discerned under pressure, yet embraced in peace. We were only given to see the step immediately before us. It was grace enough for the moment. It was hope for the days to come.

Endnotes

1. "For a Leader," from *To Bless the Space Between Us: A Book of Blessings* by John O'Donohue, copyright © 2008 by John O'Donohue. Used by permission of Doubleday, an imprint of the Knopf Doubleday Publishing Group, a division of Penguin Random House LLC. All rights reserved.
2. Quoted in: Rose Mary Dougherty, SSND, *Group Spiritual Direction, Community for Discernment*. (Paulist Press, 1995).
3. Otto Scharmer, *Theory U: Leading from the Future as It Emerges*. (Berrett-Koehler Publishers, Inc., 2009).
4. "A Big Heart Open to God: An Interview with Pope Francis," by Antonio Spadaro, SJ, *America*, September 30, 2013.

For Reflection and Dialogue

1. What caught your attention in learning of the processes used by LCWR for group decision-making? Was there anything new to you or anything which could be useful to you in the future?

2. Of the predispositions helpful for discernment, which ones would you like to deepen in your own life?

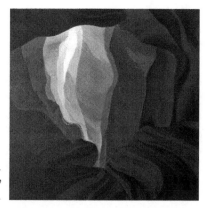

Communal discernment ...
invites us to recognize both the light and the shadow
present in who we are together.

4

Common Journey Through Diverse Paths: Developing Right Relationships in Conflictual Situations

Janet Mock, CSJ

At some thoughts one stands perplexed, especially at the sight of (human) sin,
and wonders whether one should use force or humble love.
Always decide to use humble love.
If you resolve on that once and for all, you may subdue the whole world.
Loving humility is marvelously strong, the strongest of all things
and there is nothing else like it.[1]
-- Fyodor Dostoyevsky, The Brothers Karamazov

The doctrinal assessment of the Leadership Conference of Women Religious (LCWR) was announced in 2009 and the final conversation with those representing the Congregation for the Doctrine of the Faith (CDF) took place in 2015. When the presidents and staff who held office during those years gathered to discuss whether or not to publish a book about the experience, we reached a consensus to write about what we had learned through the experience in order to honor the sacredness of the journey. And so, the questions began. What have we learned together as women and as a national organization that might have a word to offer to a national conversation about working together for the common good across varied worldviews? Is there anything from our experience that might illuminate a way forward for the US citizenry in these shadowy times? This book attempts to articulate some learnings and skills that could move a group toward civil discourse about diverse beliefs, worldviews, and values. To that end, this chapter focuses on establishing and sustaining good, authentic relationships in conflictual situations.

Human relationships at best are complicated. Add family, church, country, culture, and socioeconomic realities, and the complexities increase exponentially. The primal school of learning how to be with others is the family. Volumes have been written on the family as a social system where consciously and subconsciously we learn and act upon behaviors that reward and those which bring inevitable punishment. As we mature, we begin to sort this out and choose ways of being that reflect the way we want to live our lives. We choose friendships among people who value and love us, those who care enough to call forth our better selves. We gradually let go of trying to please people who have never had our best interests at heart. We turn our attention toward maturation and generativity, caring for the next generation and living our lives along a moral code that protects and defends all we possess for those who will come after us.

Sounds pretty simple and straightforward, doesn't it? Relationships are anything but simple and even less straightforward. The drive to be in relationship lies at the center of our being; the desire to belong, to love, and be loved takes on enormous meaning during the various seasons of life. Given different cultural values, psychological health or lack of it, moral agency, and the varied worldviews we bear and encounter throughout life, it is a miracle people can live and work together at all. And yet we do, and often well, with purpose and meaning for the common good of the larger community, be that family, neighborhood, church, nation, world, or, in the case of women and men religious, a commitment to community – religious and global.

In a summer 2017 *New York Times* op-ed column, Thomas L. Friedman was asked a question posed by a Canadian gentleman who was trying to understand what was going on in the United States: "What do you fear most these days?" Friedman replied, "I fear we're seeing the end of 'truth' – that we can't agree any more on basic facts. And I fear we're becoming Sunnis and Shiites – we call them 'Democrats' and 'Republicans,' but the sectarianism that has destroyed nation-states in the Middle East is now infecting us."

Friedman went on to quote a friend and teacher, Dov Seidman, who said, "What we are experiencing is an assault on the very foundation of our society and democracy – the twin pillars of truth and trust …. What makes us Americans is that we signed up to have a relationship with ideals that are greater than us [sic] and with truths that we agreed were so self-evident they would be the foundation of our shared journey toward a more perfect union – and of respectful disagreement along the way. We also agreed that the source of legitimate authority to govern would come from 'We the people.' But when there is no 'we' anymore, because 'we' no longer share basic truths, then there is no legitimate authority and no unifying basis for our continued association."[2]

This exchange among concerned thinkers illuminated the experience of LCWR leaders as together we reflected on our experience of the doctrinal assessment.

The prelates working at the CDF have as their mandate the protection and preservation of the patrimony of the church – the deposit of faith that we hold as Catholics. As they reviewed our writings, they concluded that we no longer held common beliefs, truths that define us as Catholic.

We women religious were stunned that our belief in that doctrine was being called into question. We did not recognize ourselves in CDF's description of us as stated in the mandate. How does one go about developing an authentic relationship with a group of people who, in our experience, took words out of context and acted against us on that misrepresentation of truth? When there is no truth, there is no trust – and consequently, no authentic relationship.

> The drive to be in relationship lies at the center of our being; the desire to belong, to love, and be loved takes on enormous meaning during the various seasons of life.

In time and through many intense conversations, we came to know first, that those representing CDF were not the actual members of the church hierarchy who had accused us of straying from the Catholic faith, though the CDF representatives supported the accusers' perception of us. Secondly, the men with whom we were speaking interpreted the way we prayed together and spoke about God and the things of God as a violation of Catholic orthodoxy. We, in turn, had spent more than 50 years as an organization, encouraging member congregations to study and pray with the documents of Vatican II which resulted in well-developed spiritualties consistent with each congregation's charism. As the organization influenced member congregations, likewise, that corporate study and prayer rooted in sound theology became the springboard for articulating evolving images of God organizationally. This articulation bore fruit in an incarnational spirituality which focuses on the Spirit alive within all of humankind and reflected in creation, and especially in the faces of those who are made poor by injustice. For us women religious, theology and spirituality are vital disciplines informing and influencing how we live our lives according to the Gospel.

We believe this is true for a number of the clerics we encountered in this process as well, and is certainly true of Pope Francis. The building of truth and consequent trust, nonetheless, took time and patience on everyone's part.

What then can be learned from the LCWR-CDF experience that might shed light on our current national reality? We offer three dimensions of forming and building relationships that we learned in the process:

- Understanding the other as a way of building trust;

- Naming and claiming what is meant by the common good;

- Choosing a way forward that reflects our better long-held values and enhances the common good of all.

Understanding the Other as a Way of Building Trust

In his simple and profound "Rules for a Dialogic Community,"[3] Marianist Brother Bernard Lee suggests the following four rules for developing and sustaining a true dialogic community:

1. When I speak, my entire reason for speaking is to give another person his/her best chance for understanding me: what I think, how I feel, where I come from, where I'd like to go, what matters to me a lot, my likes, my dislikes, etc. If I ever have the intention, while I am speaking, of convincing another person to see it my way, I have lost it. I speak not to convince, but to be understood.

2. When I listen, my entire reason for listening is to give me the best chance of understanding another person. I must hear them on their own grounds and let their words mean what they mean to them, not what they mean to me. If I start refuting or arguing when I listen (even, or especially, if it's just internal and I haven't voiced it), I have lost it.

3. Participants in true dialogic communities each agree with the others that "I will not go away from the conversation, no matter what." That gives us permission to say whatever we feel the need to say and not wonder

whether it will ruin the relationship. We're there for the long haul and we all know it.

4.   We must engage in what the philosopher Karl Jaspers calls "loving battle." If I know something that will strengthen your position against my position, and you do not know it, I must tell you. The goal is not to win an argument, but to live together in truth.

The following commentary illustrates methods employed in the LCWR-CDF ongoing conversation, using the rules suggested by Bernard Lee, SM:

1.   *When I speak, my entire reason for speaking is to give another person his/her best chance for understanding me – what I think, how I feel, where I come from, where I'd like to go, what matters to me a lot, my likes, my dislikes, etc. If I ever have the intention, while I am speaking, of convincing another person to see it my way, I have lost it. I speak not to convince, but to be understood.*

Inherent in the renewal of LCWR religious congregations was the updating and articulation of the church's Catholic Social Teaching. The three legs of the stool of social justice are education, advocacy, and direct service. Steeped in this direction and the "See, Judge, Act" methodology proposed in Pope John XXIII's 1961 encyclical, *Mater et Magistra,*[4] women religious easily fall into one or more of these ways of conversing about matters that matter. As we began to meet with representatives of CDF, we found it indispensable to listen deeply both to the hierarchy representing CDF and within ourselves as a body in order to respond from a level of deep prayer and authentic consideration of the accusations before us. We stood on 50 years of collective prayer, study, and dialogue about our life and needed time to mine the depths of what we had learned in order to speak from that well of wisdom and knowledge. We learned that through the years we had not effectively communicated what we were learning to bishops and also came to realize that some bishops simply disagreed with our research and consequent renewal of religious life.

2.   *When I listen, my entire reason for listening is to give me the best chance of understanding another person. I must hear them on their own grounds and let their words mean what they mean to them, not what they mean to me. If I start refuting or arguing when I listen (even, or especially, if it's just internal and I haven't voiced it), I have lost it.*

We LCWR officers attempted to listen carefully to the cardinals and archbishops with whom we were in dialogue in Rome and the three bishop delegates in the United States appointed to work with us to truly understand their position. In the process, we began to meet these men as brothers in Christ who held a deep commitment to Jesus Christ and the Catholic Church. This was a ground of common meaning and with some, the beginning of trust.

As we worked with one another through this difficult time, we wrestled with warnings from our colleagues and the public against trusting anyone representing CDF in this process. "Collusion with the enemy is a dangerous thing," they said. We made a conscious decision to not view the other as an enemy. We chose to stand on the common ground of our humanity, our baptism, and our vowed commitment to God and the Catholic Church in our encounters with the men representing CDF. Leaning into this positive energy enabled us to meet one another as mature adults.

It took a while to build trust. It was a conscious decision to choose to trust the men with whom we felt we could have honest conversations, to listen carefully to them and have them heard on their terms and, simultaneously, to be heard by them on ours. We chose to trust and were not disappointed nor betrayed.

What is the corollary with public discourse in American life today? The answer is a question. What structures can be put in place so that public officials and those who elect them can speak candidly with one another and be heard on their own terms? It demands a decision to trust another for the good of all; a risky step, yet indispensable for bridging the gap.

3.   *Participants in true dialogic communities each agree with the others that "I will not go away from the conversation, no matter what." That gives us permission to say whatever we feel the need to say and not wonder whether it will ruin the relationship. We're there for the long haul and we all know it.*

The commitment to stay at the table is crucial in building relationships. One of the more unlikely positive results of the CDF mandate LCWR received was that it set up a structure where we had to be "at the table" and "stay at the table" until both parties were satisfied. For us representing LCWR, honoring the integrity of both CDF and LCWR was critical to this process. There was a clear power differential in this relationship. Within the Vatican Curia, CDF protects the integrity of church doctrine. We at LCWR respect the office and sought ways to explain what we had learned as women religious through the years that supported the building up of the church. Because some of the data CDF had received in the assessment was a combination of sentences and phrases taken out of context as well as actual misinformation, we felt that the leaders in CDF were given inaccurate research, which placed them in a vulnerable situation as they talked with us. None of us wanted the office to be publicly humiliated, yet these inaccuracies were made public by CDF. In the end, it was our common love of the church and our commitment that it be all it could be that played a part in moving toward a resolution.

4. *We must engage in what the philosopher Karl Jaspers calls "loving battle." If I know something that will strengthen your position against my position, and you do not know it, I must tell you. The goal is not to win an argument, but to live together in truth.*

This degree of integrity is possible over the long run, but it takes time; time to get to know the other, time for healing, time to create an atmosphere of trust, and time for real conversation to begin in order to move to this level of dialogue. We did reach truth, as well as mutual understanding, trust, and respect and, in some cases, friendship.

These rules for dialogic community are strenuous, requiring discipline and the capacity for authentic relationship, and yet so worth the effort. They present a way through the mire of complexities in which we find ourselves in the 21st century. Commitment to the forming of relationships across diversity is a skill of inestimable value in our world today. In the 1980s, National Public Radio (NPR) ran a segment on a group in Cambridge, Massachusetts who gathered to "face the opposition." Fifteen women and men who named themselves "pro-life" met with 15 women and men who named themselves "pro-choice" for a day of sharing. They had hired facilitators and in the morning session all were asked to share why they held the positions they did. The facilitators instructed the group to hold as their primary tasks for the day "to listen and to learn." They spent the morning simply listening to one another tell why each person held the position she/he did. The entire group shared lunch together and in the afternoon they gathered again in their circle. The facilitators instructed each person in the group to think about a time when she/he had a moment of ethical doubt about the position she/he held. They then shared those experiences. The NPR report ended with the comment that at the end of the day, no one in the group changed his/her original position but they came away with a much greater understanding of why those who held differing perspectives believed what they did and each found him/herself much less judgmental of the other. Because the experiment was so compelling, NPR did

> We did reach truth, as well as mutual understanding, trust, and respect and, in some cases, friendship.

a follow-up story on this experience 30 years later and discovered that many in this original group continued to meet through the years. They were able to take concerted stands together on many issues and when they could not agree on an action step, they listened to one another in order to understand the different perspective and became good friends in the process. They had done what they were asked to do at that first meeting in the 1980s; they listened and they learned from one another. In the process, they built trust with one another. These circles of understanding are one way forward in building trust in today's complex society.

Naming and Claiming What is Meant by the Common Good

To set a context for this way forward, I draw on the wisdom of a columnist who, like others in his field, has been fearless in attempting to educate his readers about the danger we face as a nation. In the spring of 2017 *New York Times* columnist David Brooks wrote:

> Last week, two of the [White House] top advisers wrote the following in the *Wall Street Journal*:
>
>> *The President embarked on his first foreign trip with a clear-eyed outlook that the world is not a "global community" but an arena where nations, non-governmental actors and business engage and compete for advantage.*

Brooks continues:

> [This statement] asserts that selfishness is the sole driver of human affairs. It grows out of a worldview that life is a competitive struggle for gain. It implies that cooperative communities are hypocritical covers for the selfish jockeying underneath. [5]

Brooks goes on to demonstrate how this perspective explains why many people are suspicious of any cooperative global arrangement like NATO, trade agreements, or the Paris Accord on global warming. He also gives reason for the rise of various global "strongmen" in the world today.

Brooks says: "They [the strongmen] share [a] core worldview that life is nakedly a selfish struggle for money and dominance."

"The world is not a global community." Reading these words is shocking to us whose whole lives have been constituted on and oriented toward the building up of a global community. We talk about it in diverse ways: furthering the reign of God; honoring the cosmic union in which the universe was made; contributing to the common good; being part of building up our planetary household. To have that vision scorned and disregarded at a national level reveals the work ahead of us – but what is this work? What will make a difference when truth and trust are eroding to the point of a national loss of meaning?

Partisanship has always been a part of the national character of citizens of the United States. While the balance of power is built into the Constitution of the United States, the way the three branches of government work together depends largely on each party's will and ability to work across party lines, to appreciate the diverse thinking of the other and seek a fuller truth. While throughout history, partisanship often has defined the political landscape, we in the United States are now suffering with a national government that is, for the most part, split along party lines.

The common good! Of whom? My constituents? My political party? My neighborhood? Is the whole world my home or is my home -- my interests -- my whole world?

Choosing a Way Forward that Reflects Our Better Long-Held Values and Enhances the Common Good of All

*I*t is said that the Declaration of Independence was written to articulate the vision of a new country and the Constitution was penned to assure that its citizens would live from that vision. In all of us, there are opposing spirits – those that seek good and the common good of all and those that are ego-driven and sinful. The Constitution helps us live by our better angels. Similar to what the Constitution does for the nation, each religious congregation has a constitution that forms and informs its members. Each congregation has a charism, a gift to offer the People of God. This sets the vision. Our constitutions call us to embody that vision. Because LCWR is a resource serving the leadership of religious institutes of women, its bylaws hold its board and members accountable.

Our encounter with CDF called into question our fidelity to renewal as articulated in our bylaws, bylaws that were approved by another Vatican office called the Congregation for Institutes of Consecrated Life and Societies of Apostolic Life (CICLSAL). Complicating matters, that office had recently experienced a transition in leadership and the new leaders had not been informed about the CDF mandate for reform before it was presented to LCWR in 2012.

As we officers of LCWR began to move through the process of receiving the mandate and attempting conversations that could illuminate its meaning, we were aware that there were things happening that precipitated this mandate about which we were not informed – and, as it turned out, would never be informed. We did become aware, however, that duplicity was at work, as people that the previous leaders at LCWR had trusted had, in fact, betrayed that trust. We felt blind-sided and unprepared for the drama that was unleashed, as the full assessment and mandate were released to the US press moments before we had actually received these documents ourselves while meeting with CDF officials in Rome. There was reason to react, and it took discipline to listen, to seek understanding, to refuse to be either naïve or reactionary. In situations like this, there is temptation to react in kind. Drawing strength and insight from the sacred scriptures as well as wisdom from other sources, we attempted to name realities, curb anger, and seek to respond in a way that served the greater good.

The Russian novelist Fyodor Dostoyevsky writes:

> No one can judge a criminal until he recognizes that he is just such a criminal as the [one] standing before him, and that he perhaps is more than all [persons] to blame for that crime. When he understands that, he will be able to judge.

> [You are able to judge] when you take upon yourself the crime of the criminal your heart is judging, take it at once, suffer for him yourself, and let him go without reproach. If after you kiss, he goes away untouched, mocking at you, do not let that be a stumbling block to you. It shows his time has not yet come, but it will come in due course. And if not, no matter. If not he, then another in his place will understand and suffer and judge and condemn himself and the truth will be fulfilled.[6]

What were the learnings for LCWR? How could we suspend judgment until we understood what was happening? What truths did we need to hear that could improve our organization? What insults did we have to absorb in order to reach a deeper truth?

Parker Palmer, Quaker, educator, writer, activist, and founder of the Center for Courage and Renewal, talks about the need for people to "stand in the tragic gap," which he describes as "the gap between the difficult realities of life and what we know to be possible humanly" and to stand there without flipping out on either side.

Palmer continues: "To flip out on the side of too much reality is to become cynical. *It's a jungle out there and I'll find some way to survive.* Cynicism simply contributes to making the world a harder place. If you flip out on the other side into too much possibility, you become, I think, a kind of irrelevant idealist, who simply flies above the battle without ever really descending to engage it in human terms." Palmer concludes: "It is not easy to stand in the middle ground, in the space between what is and what could be. In fact, it is uncomfortable and scary. So we need communities of support where we can develop the inner strength necessary to hold both the world's reality and our hopes for the future."[7]

We at LCWR were less tempted to becoming irrelevant idealists, but squarely lured to flip out into cynicism. Holding the questions and asking deeper and deeper questions held us in the gap, which seemed to us quite tragic. Palmer's insight about needing communities of support was very relevant. Four bodies of support upon which LCWR's leaders drew mightily were our members who asked probing and insightful questions, the wise men and women with whom we consulted, religious congregations around the world, and the wider community of lay women and men locally, nationally, and internationally who prayed for and with us, wrote letters on our behalf, and gathered regularly to support us. When we received the mandate, we were afraid it would split the church. We were completely unprepared for the outpouring of support we received from our fellow lay sisters and brothers who felt a certain disenfranchisement within the church. We also received stark criticism from other laity, words we needed to take to heart and discern carefully. It seemed to us a tipping point in the life of an already divided church.

> We chose to trust and were not disappointed nor betrayed.

A decision to always hold the greater good of the People of God before us and refuse to demonize and defame the CDF were guiding lights throughout these years. In the end, this encounter between LCWR and CDF was a "presenting problem" of a much bigger and more complex situation within the hierarchy of the Catholic Church. During the years of the mandate, Pope Benedict resigned and Pope Francis was elected to the papacy. With a charter from the cardinals gathered in the 2013 conclave, a profound renewal of the Vatican

Curia began. Forces larger than LCWR created a more pastoral environment that enabled true dialogue to begin to take place. The archbishop delegate and others working directly with LCWR on behalf of CDF had already employed this way of moving forward, which was a singular grace throughout the years of the mandate.

This process gives us hope as our nation grapples with similar complexities. In the end, we believe the work of the Spirit of God saved the day. We can count on that as together we forge a future for those who will come after us. Those who are trustworthy must build alliances across the divides and the quest for common ground must be a goal as well as a strategy. The way of the future points to diversity as a norm. We must learn from one another and we must learn to respect one another. In his work, *The Primal Vision*, John V. Taylor writes:

> *Our first task in approaching another people, another culture, another religion*
> *is to take off our shoes,*
> *for the place is holy.*
> *Else we find ourselves treading on people's dreams.*
> *More serious still*
> *we may forget that God was there before we arrived.*[8]

Living through conflict is a wise mentor for all that lies ahead. In his famous book on Francis of Assisi, G.K. Chesterton points to a quality of Francis that we might emulate in our times:

> *What gave [Francis] his extraordinary power was this: that from the Pope to the beggar, from the sultan of Syria in his pavilion to the ragged robbers crawling out of the wood, there was never a [person] who looked into those brown burning eyes without being certain that Francis Bernadone was really interested in him.... Now for this particular moral and religious idea there is no external expression except courtesy.... It can only be conveyed by a certain grand manner which may be called good manners. He treated everyone like royalty. And this was really and truly the only attitude that will appeal to that part of a person to which he wished to appeal. It cannot be done by giving gold or even bread, for it is a proverb that any reveler may fling largesse in mere scorn.... No plans or proposals or efficient arrangements will give back to a broken person self-respect and a sense of speaking with an equal. One gesture will do it.*[9]

This was the quality of presence we came to expect from the archbishop delegate and others from the CDF who worked closely with him. It was, as a matter of fact, the quality we intuitively most looked for in the people with whom we consulted.

Is it any wonder that Cardinal Jorge Bergoglio chose the name Francis for these times? Through his truth-seeking, his openness, his powers of discernment, and his trust in the People of God, especially those who are poor, Pope Francis is showing us the path forward.

This chapter begins with an excerpt from *The Brothers Karamazov*, advocating the gesture of humble love rather than force in resolving matters of conflict. In the end, it was this very human, Christian, Catholic virtue on both sides of the table that enabled us to listen to one another, hear the points of conflict, and reach resolution – and in the process, develop lasting friendships.

Endnotes

1. Fyodor Dostoevsky, *The Brothers Karamozov*. Translated from the text of the Soviet Academy of Sciences edition (Leningrad 1976) by Larissa Volokhansky and Richard Pevear, North Point Press, Canada, 1990.
2. Thomas L. Friedman, *New York Times* opinion editorial, "Where Did 'We the People' Go?" June 21, 2017.
3. Bernard Lee, SM, "Rules for a Dialogic Community," part of a lecture to participants in ForMission, a program developed and sponsored by the Religious Formation Conference, Spring 2004, Oblate School of Theology, San Antonio, TX.
4. Pope John XXIII "Mater et Magistra" – encyclical published by the Vatican, May 15, 1961.
5. David Brooks, *New York Times* opinion editorial, "Donald Trump Poisons the World," June 2, 2017.
6. Ibid - Dostoevsky
7. Parker Palmer, "Standing in the Tragic Gap" – YouTube presentation; 2016 (Chapter 10 of a Courage and Renewal YouTube series)
8. John V. Taylor, *The Primal Vision*. SCM Classic Series, SCM Press; 2001.
9. G.K. Chesterton, *Francis of Assisi*. Biblio Bazaar, 2010 - a copy of a book published before 1923.

For Reflection and Dialogue

1.   Consider a conflictual situation or relationship in your life. Try to imagine how that situation might be impacted if Lee's rules for a dialogic community were applied. Which would be most challenging for you, and why?

2.   "Is the whole world my home or is my home -- my interests -- my whole world?" How would you answer that question? What does your answer say to you about your commitment to the common good?

3.   If you or an organization of which you are a part is experiencing a conflictual situation, has this chapter provided an insight into a new way forward? If so, what is that insight and what does it call for from you?

A decision to always hold the greater good of the People of God before us and refuse to demonize and defame the CDF were guiding lights throughout these years.

5

Relationships Matter:
Nonviolence and the Pressure to React

Marcia Allen, CSJ and Florence Deacon, OSF

Love alone is capable of uniting living beings
in such a way as to complete and fulfill them,
for it alone takes them and joins them by
what is deepest in themselves.
-- Pierre Teilhard de Chardin, SJ, Phenomenon of Man

"*L*ove alone is capable of uniting living beings…by what is deepest in themselves." Teilhard's words about the business of uniting living beings around what is deepest in themselves take us immediately to our journey through the process of the doctrinal assessment and the resolution of the mandate. How to respond to this event which seemed to challenge our mission and purpose as a conference, our personal and collective integrity, and our very identity? It was such that we were required to move deep into the core of our personal meaning and that of the conference itself. We began to realize that we must set aside our individuality, that egotistical self-protective shield, and begin to exercise true personhood -- openness and transparent honesty in relationships with others.

The mandate that was issued as a result of the assessment by the Congregation for the Doctrine of the Faith (CDF) of the Leadership Conference of Women Religious (LCWR) was intended as a reform of the conference with criteria that threatened its integrity. As events unfolded we were convinced that love for church and Gospel must lead us in our response. These not only ruled our hearts and loyalties but also our responses to the conclusion of the assessment and the subsequent mandate for reform.

LCWR was aware of its scrutiny by CDF from March 9, 2009 when the president of LCWR received a letter from the prefect of the CDF advising her that the CDF had appointed a US bishop to conduct a doctrinal assessment of LCWR's activities and initiatives. The presidents resolved to keep this confidential and supplied all the documents he requested. The process seemed to be proceeding normally and in an orderly fashion. He occasionally asked for additional documents and LCWR provided them. By December 2011, his work was completed and his report had been submitted to the CDF. LCWR did not receive a copy or any other notice from CDF after this.

Normalcy became chaos quite suddenly with the announcement on April 18, 2012 through the USCCB website that the investigation had ended and the final report and accompanying mandate for reform of LCWR was made public. A media firestorm erupted. Pundits and experts alike quickly took sides and gave testimony to the falsity and unfairness of the assessment or its veracity and timeliness. The media seemed to believe that its many voices could dispute and settle whether the mandate was duly earned by LCWR or unjustly imposed. Those venues were only too anxious to weigh in on the apparent conflict, make the most of it, and encourage those most intimately involved in it to engage with one another in the public forum. The temptation to do so was an ever-present reality within LCWR. The very human inclination to defend ourselves and the conference, to protest wrong judgment, error, and misinterpretation on the part of our accusers, to justify ourselves and the conference, to float on the reputations of thousands of individual sisters and hundreds of orders whose leaders were members of the conference was ever present. Realizing our own vulnerability to these less than honorable means of response we chose, rather, to respond only after careful discernment in communal contemplative silence and conversation amid the pressure to react.

Our Responsibility Unfolds

As our silence in the face of public demand for response or reaction persisted, questions arose. What were we doing in the silence? Our friends and enemies alike questioned the wisdom of this. Was it cowardice? Was it an escape? Were we too confused to respond? Were the accusations actually correct? Was the mandate for reform and its intrusiveness into the autonomy of the conference something that was needed after all? What were the real feelings of those most involved? Was there a plan that would soon be revealed? Did we, the LCWR leadership, have a *deus ex machina* that we would unveil and suddenly close the whole issue with CDF? Or was CDF getting the last word? In this apparent contest of wills, who would win?

In 2012, Easter was celebrated on April 8. We presidents, with the executive director, began to take our cues from the truths of the season. We had just celebrated that liminal interval between what was -- the crucifixion of Jesus of Galilee -- and what was to be -- resurrection and manifestation of the Christ. Liminal space. An interlude of silence, profound and lonely silence, a silence pregnant with mystery -- the seeming absolute and final end from which there is no relief and the promise remembered but as yet unfulfilled and thus a challenge to those who need proof in order to believe.

We had asked in advance of our 2012 meeting with CDF if there was any other information we could provide and were assured that CDF had no more questions or concerns. For our immediate preparation for the meeting we spent an hour in contemplative prayer. At the CDF meeting we were stunned and dismayed as we listened to the assessment report and mandate being read to us in its entirety. Although asked to respond following the reading, we had already decided that the wisest course would be to respond only after consultation and prayer. Over the next few days we completed our visits to various other curial offices and simply listened to what they said to us. Those who knew of the report and mandate encouraged us to work for unity. For example, the secretary for the Pontifical Council Promoting New Evangelization reminded us that we were in the midst of a difficult cultural crisis with one era, the era of modernity, ending and another beginning. This period of transition called not for doing, but for a moment of reflection. He said: "We need to go beyond the fragmentation... and find signs of unity." We listened to this as a subtext to our experience with the CDF. This was an added pressure for LCWR: maintain integrity while providing a bridge of relationships for the struggle ahead.

> *Realizing our own vulnerability to these less than honorable means of response we chose, rather, to respond only after careful discernment in communal contemplative silence and conversation amid the pressure to react.*

Silence. This was the silence that formed the first "strategy" of the LCWR leadership. It was neither artifice nor blueprint; rather, it was a careful and selective response to media pressure and personal inclination. It was thoughtfully framed speech that was silent about the content of conversations. It honored and was the result of prudential judgment. It was a silence that moved to contemplation before a reality too immense to comprehend much less articulate. To become mute, says the theologian Denys Turner, is to go silent and wait for a new language to express itself.[1] This happens when the enormity of circumstances renders one speechless. The enormity of the report and the mandate we received during our April visit to the CDF, and then its posting on the USCCB website where the media could easily access it before we had time to even alert our members was just such an event.

Caught in the midst of media cacophony, we began the long journey into the liminal space of response and what it would demand. Like the three Marys at the tomb, we began the journey in the deep silence of contemplation. We were stunned by the charges of doctrinal error, critiques and judgments about perceived policies of corporate dissent, our fidelity to radical feminism, and a distortion of our "faith in Jesus and his loving Father" as well as in "revealed doctrines of the Holy Trinity, the divinity of Christ, and the inspiration of Sacred Scripture." To this was added the charge that we were silent on life issues such as abortion and euthanasia. Overlooked and misinterpreted were all the ways in which the conference had attempted to create an enlightened leadership among its members in these fractious and ambiguous times. These were enormous public charges that threatened to inspire loss of public faith in the conference and its members – or loss of public faith in those who had made these charges.

Caught in the midst of media cacophony, we began the long journey into the liminal space of response and what it would demand.

Through the succeeding years, the executive director, board, and three-person presidency, who changed from year to year, each year one leaving and a new person coming, consistently renewed the values that the original three presidents had begun to work out in 2012. They had relied on the Easter liturgical season and the values illustrated in the season's scriptures. Broken hearts taught us compassion and fortitude, strengthened our determination to speak the truth, and underscored the need to guard and nurture the integrity of the conference and, most of all, to remain conscious of our own vulnerability. The scriptures sustained us as we read about the little community of Jesus' disciples fearful behind closed doors, trying to make sense of what had just happened. Our emotions paralleled those of the Easter liturgical season recalling death and resurrection, persecution, and a strengthened faith community committed to the Gospel and Jesus' words to his dispirited disciples: "Fear not, I bring you peace."

Discerning Our Response

As we reflected on how to respond as faithful women of the Gospel we were heartened by the thousands of letters of support and encouragement. Many also contained advice and protests of the injustice of the charges and poignant stories of their own experiences. We knew that we had to recapture our true identity -- personally, as well as that of the conference leadership and of the conference itself.

We also had to establish the principles on which we would base our actions. Over time we consulted many experts (theologians, canonists, psychologists, systems analysts, communications and media consultants, and learned friends), the members themselves, and various clergy in order to make a pathway through the dark night that was both personal and communal for ourselves and for the members individually and as a conference.

As we began to develop our operational values we knew some things almost intuitively:

- Although a very public event we would not carry out the conflict in the media.
- We would refuse to contribute to a climate of polarization; we would attempt to build bridges.
- Our response would be framed in the context of Vatican II.
- We would claim our moral authority - personally and communally.
- All decisions would be preceded by contemplative prayer - privately and communally.
- We would keep in mind that this was bigger than ourselves and had implications for a wider world.
- Non-negotiable values were:
  - Listen deeply before speaking or writing.
  - Preserve the dignity and integrity of both parties, LCWR and CDF.
  - Frame every conversation in the rules of dialogue.
  - Maintain necessary boundaries.
  - Consult with experts and stakeholders on a continuing basis.

- Process emotions and feelings first for always more cogent self-knowledge.
- Carry out the ordinary work of the conference

From this time forward the presidency, executive director, staff, national board, and membership were deeply involved in a transformational journey, both pragmatic and spiritual, that was guided by the firm principles of nonviolence, dialogue, and personal and communal integrity. To this end we turned down dozens of requests for media comment. Some few invitations were accepted but with carefully discerned messages, never revealing content of conversations. As one president observed, "Even though we clearly stated we would not talk about the doctrinal assessment in live interviews, we had to be very nimble to sidestep the topic politely."

A facilitator was engaged to help us process our feelings and emotions. The objective of this process, which was repeated several times after a conversation with CDF or a CDF remark in the media, was to create interior freedom. Not to overstate the obvious, but as a matter of fact, the temptation to justify ourselves publicly was always present. So many of the charges were egregious misrepresentations of facts; however, a lifetime of discernment and living out the spiritual life had taught us that self-knowledge reveals the redeeming need for compassion and forgiveness -- beginning with oneself. A template of the general process used and adapted to the circumstances follows:

- Engage in a period of silence.
- Invite each person to share from her heart how she is feeling.
- Engage in a second period of silence reflecting on: What did I hear in the group sharing?
- Invite each person to share with the whole group: What did I hear in our sharing?
- Process the group sharing together by completing any or all of these statements:
    - At this point in our gathering, the feelings I am aware of are ….
    - The feeling drawing my attention most strongly is … because ….
    - A moment in the meeting that touched me or gave me hope was … because ….
- Conclude the process by engaging in questions such as:
    - What is the best outcome? What is the hoped-for outcome?
    - What does (here name the appropriate person or group) need to know or do?

We engaged this process or some form of it repeatedly among ourselves as well as at the LCWR board meetings, LCWR regional meetings, and annual assemblies. This process created a compassionate heart, a realization of personal and communal limitations, the sheer humanness of the whole situation, and an awareness of the need for forgiveness of self and others. It opened the door for a supportive community that desired against all odds to move toward reconciliation rather than self-righteousness.

Following the April 2012 meeting with CDF we processed this meeting with the LCWR board and acted on the cardinal prefect's invitation to report back to CDF if we thought the assessment needed to be re-evaluated. The board decided that the president and executive director would return to speak with the cardinal prefect about the deficiencies in the process and where they thought the assessment was not accurate. Following this meeting LCWR president Pat Farrell, OSF commented to the press: "It was an open meeting and we were able to directly express our concerns to [CDF prefect] Cardinal Levada, and [archbishop delegate] Archbishop Sartain."[2] The CDF prefect, on the other hand, described this conversation as "a dialogue with the deaf."[3]

Astounded by his public comment, we presidents and the board began once more the process toward deeper awareness of the larger reality. Once again we resolved to continue in honest, transparent dialogue with the members of CDF. The process strengthened each of us in her own identity and we were able to move once again into bold and transparent, trustful, and honest dialogue with CDF members. We were also able to maintain the resolution to keep the substance of the conflict out of the media no matter the outrageous assumptions present there from time to time.

The assessment report outlined the problematic areas that CDF found in the documents and practices of LCWR.[4] The introduction called for "ecclesial communion" characterized by "allegiance of mind and heart to the Magisterium of the Bishops, an allegiance which must be lived honestly and clearly testified to before the People of God by all consecrated persons, especially those involved in theological research, teaching, publishing, catechesis and the use of the means of social communication." Other sections of the report decried LCWR's silence and inaction in the face of error, "given its responsibility to support a vision of religious life in harmony with that of the Church and to promote a solid doctrinal basis for religious life."

The mandate had as its purpose the reform of LCWR through a process of review and conformity to the teachings and discipline of the church and the

Holy See, through CDF. Three bishops would review, guide, and approve the work of LCWR where necessary. The archbishop delegate was to report to CDF, which would inform and consult with the Congregation for Institutes of Consecrated Life and Societies of Apostolic Life (CICLSAL) and the Congregation for Bishops. This mandate was to be followed for three to five years as deemed necessary with the archbishop delegate overseeing the process. All this was in hopes that the Holy See was offering "an important contribution to the future of religious life in the Church in the United States." Problematic in the whole document was that much of the criticism cited and the reform required was either the result of misunderstandings or outside LCWR's own mission and purpose.

The archbishop delegate's appointment to oversee the "reform of the LCWR" meant that he would see that the mandate was carried out. He became the bridge between CDF and LCWR in the work toward resolution and reconciliation. In his remarks about his new assignment he expressed a desire to proceed in an "atmosphere of prayer and respectful dialogue ..." and to "work toward clearing up any misunderstandings," while remaining "truly hopeful that we will work together without compromising Church teaching or the important role of the LCWR."[5] The archbishop entered into his task with open curiosity about the mission and activities of LCWR. He was invited to LCWR board meetings and to the 2013 and 2014 annual assemblies. During the 2013 assembly he was invited to listen to the members as they spoke from the floor. They communicated their frustration and pain about being misjudged and misinterpreted.

> We believe that the ongoing conversations between CDF and LCWR may model a way of relating that only deepens and strengthens our capacity to serve a world in desperate need of our care and service.

By 2014 the prefect of CDF had been replaced (July 2, 2012). Pope Benedict had resigned and Cardinal Jorge Mario Bergoglio, SJ of Argentina had become Pope Francis (March 16, 2013). It was difficult, however, to know if these appointments would have an impact on the relationship between LCWR and CDF.

By this time we had processed the mandate with the board and the members in the regions and in assembly. The conference was determined to "stay at the table," maintain its integrity, exercise autonomy in choosing speakers and programs, remain honest and not "sugarcoat" what was happening, keep the members apprised of events, and continue to build relationships.

The Faith Journey

*A*t the annual meeting with CDF in April 2014 one of the members of CDF articulated an insight about the conflicted relationship between LCWR and CDF which they recognized had endured over decades: "A feeling arose about LCWR which became institutionalized." This insight resulted when we explained our reasons for actions which CDF had described as defiant. At once understanding opened for both sides along with potential for bridging what was recognized as a "cultural chasm."[6] Despite this apparent leap toward reconciliation, immediately after the meeting, the CDF prefect's harsh and condemnatory opening remarks about LCWR, made as the meeting began, were released to the public and widely communicated by the press, without any mention of the positive movement of the meeting. These unexplained remarks only deepened the tentativeness of the forward movement and further incensed public opinion.

This left us with feelings of disillusionment, discouragement, and frustration. In August the LCWR presidency and executive director tried to make sense of the CDF meeting and its aftermath with the archbishop delegate. We discussed again our lack of confidence in the doctrinal assessment process, our belief that many of the conclusions were unsubstantiated, and pointed out that censorship isn't part of the American culture. He observed that we were having the same conversation we had been having for the past three years.

The process seemed to be at an impasse, but the LCWR assembly and board agreed to continue the conversation as "an expression of hope that new ways may be created within the church for healthy discussion of differences." Stressing its wider importance, they explained, "We believe that the ongoing conversations between CDF and LCWR may model a way of relating that only deepens and strengthens our capacity to serve a world in desperate need of our care and service."[7]

Then CICLSAL closed a parallel review it was conducting of the lives of US apostolic Catholic sisters called an apostolic visitation in December 2014 and CDF agreed to a resolution of the mandate by April 2015. Together we, the LCWR leadership, and the archbishop delegate, along with a representative from CDF, developed a joint statement bringing the conflict to resolution. Both CDF and LCWR leaders and the archbishop delegate signed the report at their April 2015 meeting in Rome. The archbishop delegate's approach can be summed up by his fidelity to dialogue coupled with LCWR's practice of contemplative prayer and dialogue that we had consciously developed from the beginning of our work together. This journey ended in mutual understanding and friendship, deepened love for the church and religious life, and the preservation of the integrity of both CDF and LCWR.

In retrospect we might ask what actually happened. In the six years from the announcement of the doctrinal assessment in March 2009 and its denouement in April 2015, what were the overall effects of what some have called "strategies" that succeeded for LCWR? Two seem obvious. The first is that what occurred during those six years was a personal and communal faith journey. The process undergone by those in the LCWR leadership and in the conference itself bore all the earmarks of deepening relationships with God, with ourselves as leaders, with church authorities and, in this case, with the conference itself. This process, a faith journey, was proceeding on an even keel over years of developmental growth and a feeling of confidence about LCWR's engagement in its commitments to its membership. Internal growth and development of global awareness and transformational consciousness were trademarks of the members of the conference and the developmental stages in which the conference was engaging.

> *This kind of listening, although often painful and difficult, began to create deeper and wider spaces in which dialogue could take place.*

Suddenly this process was interrupted by the doctrinal assessment report and the mandate. The disjuncture created in LCWR a cloud of doubt about its own identity and forced both the presidency and the members to work through a self-examination that included processes of self-giving and self-sacrifice in the private sphere and the public arena. Exposure to the vicissitudes of public opinion as well as church censure created a forum in which certainty dissolved. In August 2012 when the prospects of a dialogue or any kind of understanding seemed most impossible and the temptation was to retaliate in self-aggrandizing arguments of righteousness, the conference members in assembly chose a counterintuitive measure. The assembly participants invoked the Holy Spirit and prayed: "We abandon ourselves into your hands, O God. Keep our hearts soft and our minds open, as we wait for the truth of this moment to reveal itself."[8] Praying for soft hearts in tough times seems a doubtful strategy but it does denote the disposition of the conference to be open to the action of God in their midst -- and in the midst of the trouble they were experiencing. This predisposition to grace was the underpinning of the faith journey through the years, and it manifested in a stance of compassion rather than the violence that the event would seem naturally to evoke.

The second "strategy" employed during these six years might be described as deliberately nonviolent according to methods recognized as standard in any conflict. Scilla Elworthy, an experienced theorist and practitioner of nonviolent means to settle disputes among peoples around the globe, proposes a framework that enables those engaged in conflict to come to peaceful terms.[9] She suggests that there is a certain "feminine intelligence," available to men as well as women, that enables conflicted parties to experience a shift in consciousness and thus bring about reconciliation and peace. Elworthy's framework includes compassion, inclusivity, listening, interconnectedness, and regeneration.

By the same token, LCWR, as a conference and as members, employed basic attitudes found in Elworthy's framework: humility and openness, curiosity and patience, fidelity to the process and one another, resilience, courage, and generosity of person. Observers saw these attitudes emerge and unfold, mature, and become effective as the years wore on. The internal dynamic for LCWR's purposes was that relationships matter: relationships with God, self, the Catholic Church, the conference and its mission and members, CDF, the officers of CDF, and the bishop delegates.

Relationships Matter

The processes employed by LCWR leadership and members to begin with were those that led them toward compassion -- compassion toward themselves and then toward CDF. This compassion was the foundation for building relationships. Our goal was the strength of purposeful encounters in our conversations with CDF members and the appointed delegate. From the beginning the LCWR leadership was careful to include all who might enable us to deal constructively with the assessment as well as those who were determined to work their will on the conference. And compassion was the coin with which we entered every exchange. Listening carefully, we first opened our ears to the literal spoken word and then in the silence of our hearts we processed the meaning of what we had heard. This kind of listening, although often painful and difficult, began to create deeper and wider spaces in which dialogue could take place. Relationships mattered. Both leaders and members of the conference understood the implicate order in which we lived: all were connected by an intrinsic bond that made us one whether we would accept it or not. The point here is that we did accept it and we acted on it. Threats to the bonds of relationship always outweighed personal cost.

Nor did we ever forget what Elworthy would call regenerative power, that is, the implications of our actions and words for the larger church or for the world itself. Although we were in the immediate sphere wholly preoccupied with the needs of our relationship with CDF, we also knew that whatever we did affected the greater world. In her 2014 address to the annual LCWR assembly, LCWR president Florence Deacon, OSF presented reflections on what it means to be a faithful woman of the church as a framework for a way forward in LCWR's relationships with church leaders. Referring to LCWR's doctrinal assessment, she concluded, "Our situation reflects larger questions and concerns such as the ongoing implementation of the Second Vatican Council; the ecclesial roles of women religious and of the laity, especially women; understandings of authority, faithful dissent, and obedience; and the need for spaces where honest, probing questions about faith and belief can be raised and discussed."[10]

The now deceased theologian and philosopher Beatrice Bruteau distinguishes between individual and person.[11] Whereas an individual is an individual substance of a rational nature with boundaried self-protective devices, a person (from the Latin *per* and *sonare* meaning "to sound through") is one in whom there is a fundamental openness. A person is a replication of the Trinitarian *perichoresis* in that persons are not made of building blocks but complicated webs of energy relations. "[I]nterconnectedness lies at the core of all that exists," Bruteau asserts.[12] In other words personhood is fulfilled in relationships and communion. After lifetimes shaped by theological studies and communal practices, the leadership of LCWR had an intuitive comprehension of the real meaning of person -- our own personhood -- in that it was through our own openness to potential communion that we were able to continue to approach CDF with the intent and hope for dialogue. Eventually, through our communion with the archbishop delegate, this goal with CDF was realized. Our efforts were regenerative. We hoped that our efforts would encourage future dialogue within the church as a whole.

The words of LCWR president Pat Farrell, OSF to the LCWR assembly in 2013 expressed this. In the midst of the polarization in the Catholic Church she emphasized the importance to "really see another person and to really allow ourselves to be seen.... Expressing what we really think and feel, with transparency and vulnerability, is for the brave of heart. It is, however, what we are being asked to do in our current conflict. All of a sudden the world is looking to us. In response, we keep calling ourselves and one another to truthfulness and integrity, to a thoughtful sorting out of what that looks like concretely." [13]

At the end of it all the CDF prefect said: "...the Congregation (CDF) is confident that LCWR has made clear its mission to support its member Institutes by fostering a vision of religious life that is centered on the Person of Jesus Christ and is rooted in the Tradition of the Church. It is this vision that makes religious women and men radical witnesses to the Gospel, and therefore, is essential for the flourishing of religious life in the Church."[14]

The archbishop delegate summed it up this way: "Our work together was undertaken in an atmosphere of love for the Church and profound respect for the critical place of religious life in the United States, and the very fact of such substantive dialogue between bishops and religious women has been mutually beneficial and a blessing from the Lord.... The other two Bishop Delegates and I are grateful for the opportunity to be involved in such a fruitful dialogue."[15]

> ... we relied on personal and communal inner work that animated our refusal to leave the table, carry out disagreements in the media, or engage in self-serving rhetoric of complaints and blaming.

The LCWR board members also expressed their gratitude and hope: "Our greatest desire now is that the positive outcome of these years of intense work at building relationships, establishing trust, inviting questions, and creating spaces for honest conversations -- even on topics that can be divisive -- will serve as a source of hope to others within the church and the world. Clearly, such work is demanding and difficult, but in this age of intolerance of differences and growing polarities, it may be one of the most indispensable tasks of these times."[16]

LCWR's best strategy, as it turned out, was a real expression of personhood and an expression of love that is self-gift for the benefit of others. This led to partnerships in a continuing conversation that became open and honest dialogue about real concerns; reverenced the essential person within the individuals with whom we engaged; and fostered truth-seeking and authentic respect for the roles each group played in the life of the church. To accomplish this, we relied on personal and communal inner work that animated our refusal to leave the table, carry out disagreements in the media, or engage in self-serving rhetoric of complaints and blaming. By the same token we could risk personal dignity by going forward with conversations in hard times, and continue a policy of honesty and openness in all communication. Above all we, both leaders and members, kept to our resolution to be faithful to continuous contemplative prayer and discernment -- personally and communally. Of the process --"for however long the night" truly it can be said that

> *"Love alone is capable of uniting human beings*
> *in such a way as to complete and fulfill them,*
> *for it alone takes them and joins them by*
> *what is deepest in themselves."*
> *-- Pierre Teilhard de Chardin, SJ*

Relationships matter

For Reflection and Dialogue

1. Consider what you've learned from this essay. How might it help you now or in the future?
2. Are there blocks in your life that prevent you from interacting with compassion towards another? If so, can you name them? What difference does naming them make in your life?
3. "Sing a new song..." cries the psalmist (Ps 149). How have your past experiences turned into new songs that you might not have imagined at the time – or might be called "new songs" as you ruminate on them now?

Endnotes

1. Denys Turner, *Eros and Allegory*. Kalamazoo, MI: Cistercian Publications, 1995, p. 61.

2. LCWR Statement on Meeting with CDF on June 12, 2012

3. "Vatican Official Warns of 'Dialogue with the Deaf,'" Interview of Cardinal Levada by John L. Allen, Jr. for the *National Catholic Reporter*, June 12, 2012.

4. Congregatio Pro Doctrina Fidei (Congregation for the Doctrine of the Faith). "Doctrinal Assessment of the Leadership Conference of Women Religious," April 2012.

5. Statement by Archbishop J. Peter Sartain regarding LCWR, quoted from the USC-CB website, August 12, 2012.

6. Sharon Holland, IHM. In her presidential address at the LCWR annual assembly in August 2015 Sharon described the misunderstandings that led to the doctrinal assessment as a "cultural chasm."

7. Press statement issued by LCWR summarizing the annual assembly of 2014.

8. *National Catholic Reporter*: "LCWR 'gathers collective wisdom' of members to discern next steps," by Joshua J. McElwee, August 8, 2012

9. Scilla Elworthy. "Dealing With the Darkness of What Humans Do to Humans," *Kosmos Journal*, published by Kosmos Associates, Inc. (www.kosmosjournal.org: kosmosjournal.org); Spring /Summer 2017, pp 4 - 7.

10. Florence Deacon, OSF, Presidential Address to Annual LCWR Assembly, 2014.

11. Ilia Delio, OSF. "Evolution toward Personhood," *Personal Transformation and a New Creation*. Maryknoll, NY: Orbis Books, 2016, 114. Quoting from *The Grand Option: Personal Transformation and a New Creation* by Beatrice Bruteau. Notre Dame, IN: University of Notre Dame Press, 2001, 143.

12. Ibid, 115.

13. Pat Farrell, OSF, acceptance speech for LCWR Outstanding Leadership Award, August 2013.

14. Joint Press release following April 16, 2015 meeting of LCWR and CDF officials.

15. Ibid.

16. Sharon Holland, IHM; Marcia Allen, CSJ; Carol Zinn, SSJ; Joan Steadman, CSC, "Statement of the LCWR Officers on the CDF Doctrinal Assessment and Conclusion of the Mandate," August 2015.

6

A Tapestry of Contrasting Colors:
Living with Polarization, Differences, and Impasse

Pat Farrell, OSF

Oh God, be the weaver of our future.
Guide the threads that we hold in our hands,
for we see only part of the pattern,
your design for our many-colored strands.[1]
--Carol Hoverman, OSF

In 2009, then LCWR president J. Lora Dambroski, OSF, received an unexpected letter from Cardinal William Levada, prefect of the Congregation for the Doctrine of the Faith, announcing a decision to conduct a doctrinal assessment of LCWR. Though the letter came as a surprise, it also reflected the climate of contrasts and tensions in which US women religious found themselves immersed. In 2009 change was in the air. Barack Obama assumed the presidency, was awarded the Nobel Peace Prize, and initiated a controversial stimulus package to inject life into an economy on the brink of a depression. He attempted to govern in the oppositional environment of a Congress explicitly determined to block his every effort.[2]

Catholic church events included the USCCB's issuance of a statement of support for the bishop of Fort Wayne-South Bend, Indiana who had come under public criticism for protesting Notre Dame's honoring of President Obama. The local bishop of Phoenix declared St. Joseph's Hospital and Medical Center to be no longer Catholic. An unprecedented large-scale visitation of all apostolic women's religious congregations had been initiated by the Vatican and sisters across the country were discerning how to respond. Such controversies were iconic of a whole spectrum of polemics within the US church.

Clearly, contrasting mentalities were on display in both church and civil society. Strands of differing viewpoints seemed only to diverge further during the years that followed. Growing polarization and mistrust in the US church and political milieu did not provide conditions for the kind of dialogue needed to weave a greater unity. There seemed to be a large-scale breakdown in communication. Confirmation bias (the tendency to interpret new evidence as confirmation of one's existing beliefs), though real, was little recognized. In both civic and religious arenas people tended to limit their dialogue to conversation with other like-minded people, living then in parallel theoretical worlds, seldom converging in genuine encounter or thoughtful dialogue. It was at this difficult juncture in 2009 that LCWR was thrust into the CDF doctrinal assessment process and was quietly formulating a response.

Then on April 18, 2012 news broke of the Vatican's mandate to reform LCWR. Messages of concern and solidarity came flooding in to our national office from all over the world. We soon witnessed a groundswell of both organized and spontaneous actions: internet campaigns, demonstrations, public statements. Media interest was surprisingly sustained, far beyond anything we could have anticipated.

From within the communication deluge, themes emerged which sparked particularly thoughtful reflection by the LCWR leadership. We heard expressions such as "tipping point" and "defining moment." There were many references to a critical juncture in church history, a tension between conscience and obedience, an urgent need for dialogue, an escalating polarization. There were poignant expressions of deep love for the church in the midst of pain and alienation, as well as some hopes pinned on LCWR to respond to the mandate in a way that might help to bridge the divide. What was happening to women religious seemed to reflect and validate the pain experienced by much of the laity.

In general, the overarching backdrop of conflict reflected the breaking down of one era and the emergence of another. We were living a tug-of-war between the desire to preserve long-held values, traditions, and institutions and the impulse to reach toward emerging alternatives. More specifically, LCWR was embroiled in a clash with church authorities which touched into the deep concerns of a much broader public, though CDF saw it as very specific and limited to LCWR itself. The prevailing ecclesial environment was one in which expression of valid differences often carried judgment concerning loyalty, orthodoxy, legitimacy. The moment suggested an urgent need to weave the contrasting colors of that tension into a tapestry with some coherent pattern.

This polarization in the US Catholic Church was our context, one we felt keenly and one which mattered a great deal to us. As women religious, our love for the church, though questioned by some, was deep and undeniable for us. The mystical, prophetic charism of religious life emerged within the church, a gift in service to the church and the world. To feel apart from or at odds with the institutional church was painful and unacceptable. The stakes were high for us. It was very important to manage well the mandate given to us, for ourselves and for the church as a whole.

None of us could claim immunity from the human realities of ego and shadow. The differences among us added to the panorama of complexity and gave no assurance of a favorable outcome.

Those of us who publicly represented LCWR would likely admit to bumping into both the best and the worst of ourselves. We universally discovered strengths we didn't know we had. Words of wisdom and generosity of spirit surfaced when needed from somewhere beyond the small self. Yet vulnerabilities were in evidence and frustration was often near the surface of our responses. None of us could claim immunity from the human realities of ego and shadow. The differences among us added to the panorama of complexity and gave no assurance of a favorable outcome. There were difficulties at every level.

LCWR leadership, though nationally representative and quite united, was not of a single mind. What approach should we take? What would be the best tone to strike, and the best timing of our responses? How could we be true to ourselves, faithful to the Gospel and the church? What did integrity look like in specific terms? Who should best do what? What was this historical moment asking of us, what prophetic response, what transformation? How were we to manage relationships? What should be made public and what held confidential? It was a challenge to speak with one voice, though clearly, we could not do otherwise.

At the level of LCWR members, the fluidity of membership guaranteed little continuity. With regular elections of congregational leaders, the membership of LCWR changes by about one-third every year. Many leaders were new or began their LCWR participation midstream in the doctrinal assessment process. Additionally, members represented differing congregational cultures, histories, and mindsets, coloring their attitudes and expectations about how best to maneuver the crisis of the doctrinal assessment. Nonetheless, the shared values, history, and lifestyle of US women religious had created a longstanding, solid base of unity. An amazingly deep solidarity prevailed, though the universe of differences among us did not allow us to presuppose such a grace.

The differences we experienced with church hierarchy suggested misunderstanding, insufficient communication, and impressions of LCWR that seemed to have become entrenched and difficult to change. A certain normal, creative tension between consecrated life and hierarchy is to be expected, the two representing complementary charisms given for the sake of the church. Yet the friction exhibited by the doctrinal assessment reflected something deeper. US women religious had gradually lived into a post-Vatican II re-visioning and understanding of authority and obedience, favoring a decentralized, participative model not mirrored in the institutional church's exercise of leadership. Without considerable dialogue it would be easy for either group to misinterpret the other. Yet structured avenues for conversation were few and the frequency and quality of communication needed for greater mutual understanding were inadequate, despite our official connections with the USCCB and the annual visit to Vatican offices by LCWR leadership in an attempt to keep channels of communication open.

LCWR responded to the CDF mandate with a commitment to enter into dialogue with the bishop delegates assigned to implement the process, up to the point at which LCWR would see its integrity compromised. Many conversations and processes ensued, some with greater ease than others. Eventually, however, the process stalemated in an impasse for which there was no evident way forward. It was a moment of great disillusionment for the LCWR presidents and executive director who had been so intensely engaged in the dialogue. With no apparent way to proceed in good faith, there was little to do but to pray, to wait, to trust. We had done what we could, and there was a certain peace that came with that recognition, despite the deep pain and frustration.

In our prayer and reflection, significant insights surfaced which helped us to find meaning in the midst of what felt like gridlock. We began to think of our situation within a global perspective. Countries in protracted war situations could see no way forward either. If our expectation was that the Syrians, or the Israelis and Palestinians stay at the table, could we, in solidarity, do anything less? If our hope was for Democrats and Republicans to find some bi-partisan space from which to govern, could we not persist in searching for common ground? If we still dreamt of a church with open dialogue among laity and hierarchy, could we not contribute on our part a vulnerable honesty and thoughtful restraint in ongoing conversation with bishop delegates?

We came to see that formulating our response to the doctrinal assessment was, actually, the current mission of LCWR, and a very important work of the conference. Perhaps the leadership most needed in the church and the world now was to stand in the midst of apparently irresolvable conflict with perseverance and hope. Was this our new call? Was this the work of leadership to which we were being summoned? The Swiss psychologist Maria Louisa von Franz affirmed that if we can stay with the tension of opposites long enough we can sometimes be the container within which divine opposites come together and give birth to a new reality. What emerged in us was the desire to do just that. We would see the doctrinal assessment process through to the end, trusting that loose strands seemingly going nowhere were being woven into some unseen pattern by the divine energy carrying us.

Once the crisis of the LCWR mandate had been resolved, LCWR leaders reflected on our lived experience of it. With the greater vision afforded by hindsight, we have recognized together what had been helpful, while not always evident in the moment. Paradoxically, what seemed most difficult and what was most helpful were at times one and the same thing. The CDF mandate was a crisis for LCWR, presenting both danger and opportunity simultaneously, those contrasting colors ultimately woven into a tapestry of unforeseen design. Following are a few examples of what was both problematic and fortuitous.

The Public Nature of the Mandate

It had not been the choice of LCWR leadership to make public the doctrinal assessment process initiated by CDF. Nor did we have any inclination to allow media to become the forum in which to conduct the delicate dialogue that was needed. However, once widespread interest had gathered, the public outpouring of both abundant support for women religious as well as indignation with the mandate itself revealed the sympathies and concerns of much of the US Catholic laity.

While the pressure of so much public attention greatly complicated the process for us, there were ways in which it was helpful. The eyes of the world were suddenly upon us, and while we could only speak for ourselves, the broad feedback we received communicated that our dilemma carried the pain and hopes of a much broader church. The public nature of this mandate was a summons to respond carefully, from the best collective self that could be coalesced among our members. It was a summons to prayerful soul searching, to creative grappling with both long-standing and immediate tensions. It steered us all more deeply into prayer and honest dialogue, with one another as well as with officially assigned interlocutors. In a certain sense it called forth the best in us.

Our Years of Lived Experience of Religious Life

The disciplines and patterns inherent in religious life simply form the fabric of our being and were what we consciously or unconsciously brought to the doctrinal assessment proceedings. Religious life is different in structure and function from the structures and functions of the clergy and church hierarchy. Canon law guarantees a certain measure of autonomy to each religious institute in the interest of safeguarding the integrity of its charismatic and prophetic nature, its gift to the church. LCWR is a forum of support and exchange for leaders in religious life but does not exercise authority over members. Congregational leadership is internally designated by each institute, assuring its self-governance. Religious institutes are self-financed and self-directed. Structures are in place for religious congregations to live in communion with but not to be controlled by local church authorities. Not surprisingly, there have been times when interactions between hierarchy and congregational leaders have not been in harmony.

On the other hand, our years of lived experience of religious life were the strength we brought to the crisis of the doctrinal assessment. Our lives of community, decentralized exercise of authority and obedience, and prayer uniquely prepared LCWR to respond as we did to polarization, differences, and impasse.

1. Community

Our life commitment as religious is not only to God but to one another. We are bound in community to the same women for the duration of a lifetime. Differences are ever-present, and we cannot escape them if we are to have any quality of life together. Community living is a school for honing communication skills and relational abilities. Over the last 50 years many learnings have been forged in facing the continual changes in religious life. It has not been easy to manage community processes with large groups of women who had found their voices and were not shy about making them heard. We learned to value differences partly because we had to. In the process, we discovered the depth of wisdom that arises when each divergent voice is allowed to be heard. Out of that experience, we know the impoverishment for the church that results from inadequate mechanisms for encouraging the expression of minority viewpoints especially from laity and religious.

Because of our community life, we came into the experience of the doctrinal assessment with a strong network of solidarity and support, both nationally and in each of our individual congregations. The presidents and executive director, together with the national board, debriefed and strategized together, laughed and cried together, disagreed and affirmed one another, while forging bonds of friendship and mutual respect. We were able to draw on the variety of experiences, life skills, and professional competencies represented in the diversity of backgrounds among us. The doctrinal assessment LCWR faced only served to deepen our connection with one another.

Locally, each of us felt abundantly supported by our own sisters. It was not uncommon for any one of us in the LCWR presidency to return from a tense meeting and to walk into the motherhouse dining room to the applause of the gathered community, to walk into our offices to find flowers or messages of support, to walk into chapel and receive special prayers of blessing. Without the spiritual and emotional support that is part of life in community our experience would have been much more difficult. We were never alone.

2. Participative structures for decision-making

We moved into decision-making in response to the doctrinal assessment out of much accumulated experience of how to listen together for the movement of the Spirit. We have learned a lot over the years about staying with ambiguity, listening long and attentively, discovering a way forward together. The path towards more inclusive decision-making has been slowly developing over a long time. For more than 50 years now US women religious' congregations have been experimenting with both a renewed interpretation as well as different structures for the exercise of authority and obedience. While the fruits of that process have by no means been uniform among congregations across the country, important commonalities can be seen. The focus universally shifted to the importance of personal and communal discernment and to more collective, participative structures that supported that dynamic. These changes reflect 50 years of the post-Vatican II commitment of much of religious life to the ongoing growth and maturity of women religious, encouraging more egalitarian adult relational dynamics, personal responsibility, and prayerfully discerned decisions.

Many creative designs have been employed in processes of communal discernment to gather the wisdom of an entire congregation in identifying future directions. In the last several years the focus has moved in the direction of contemplative group discernment, attuning entire communities to the movement of God's Spirit among them. Both LCWR as well as individual congregations have been learning how to gather the great diversity of persons and positions and weave the differences into a peaceful overall direction, if not consensus. Though it is a work in progress, we have been discovering how to modulate strong voices and assure that the quieter ones or the minority opinions are safely received and allowed to influence group decisions. Such processes tend to proceed in peace and yield wise outcomes.

> Though it is a work in progress, we have been discovering how to modulate strong voices and assure that the quieter ones or the minority opinions are safely received and allowed to influence group decisions.

Living into more participative structures and discerning processes has helped our congregations move through times of massive change together. It has not been easy. We are still learning. But the process has been enriching and most of us can no longer imagine functioning within more hierarchical frameworks of decision-making.

The institutional church has not undergone the same re-visioning of structures of authority and obedience. Consequently, related misunderstanding and judgment made their way into doctrinal assessment conversations. We found ourselves speaking different languages concerning authority and obedience, which at times complicated our efforts toward mutual understanding.

For LCWR, however, the participative structures of the national conference as well as learned processes of group discernment were invaluable in moving through the doctrinal assessment process as an undivided whole. Another chapter of this book describes in greater detail the procedures used at critical moments to manage differences and be able to speak with one voice. The process as such merits close examination. It sheds light on how the conference was able to weave together a single response from the multi-colored strands of its members.

3. Prayer

Perhaps more than any other constitutive element of our lives as religious, the practice of prayer helped us to be somewhat at peace with differences, polarization, and impasse. When there was no clear way forward, the only way was down, in surrender to the Presence at the core of each of us and within all of reality. From that inner space it was easier to recognize that more was happening than we could perceive at any given moment and that it didn't all depend on us. A hidden divine movement was at work in the whole of the situation and could be trusted. Our God who draws the human family forward toward greater life and wholeness was at work in the process we were living, beyond what we could know. We learned that as we gave ourselves over to what was being asked of us for the greater good, we would be given what we needed.

And what we needed then, now, and always was a deepening capacity to love: to love all that manifested as messy, broken, or divisive. We needed the inner stillness to live in God's presence and to be led from there into a transformation not of our own making. We needed to be given compassionate hearts of flesh stretched beyond barriers we didn't know we had erected and were incapable on our own of dismantling. We needed to surrender our hearts and minds to God. That place of prayer was a familiar home to each of us, the grounding of our personal and communal living of religious life. It was the greatest resource we brought to a critical moment.

Walking the path of the doctrinal assessment was a spiritual journey and indeed a walk in the dark. We could see only part of the pattern, the design, of threads being somehow drawn together, unfinished and uncertain. Each of us was being invited to some form of transformation: to a deeper inner freedom concerning the outcome of the doctrinal assessment; to a greater trust in God, in ourselves, in one another; to a larger capacity for relationship-building, truth-telling, and genuine humility. Only God at work in us could do such things.

> *And when we finish needing to be right,*
> *a small door opens, close to earth,*
> *close to moss and humus.*
> *Stoop low to enter.*
> *-- Regina Bechtle, SC*

Endnotes

1. Song by Carol Hoverman, OSF from the congregational songbook, *Sing Joyfully* of the Sisters of St. Francis of Dubuque, Iowa.
2. "The GOP's no-compromise pledge" by Andy Barr, *Politico*, October 28, 2010. www.politico.com/story/2010/10/the-gops-no-compromise-pledge-044311

For Reflection and Dialogue

1. We named some of the strengths that we brought to our organization's experience of crisis. What strengths do you carry that you can call upon in difficult times in your life?

2. What insights have come to you under duress which have illumined your living? How have they served you in differing situations?

A hidden divine movement was at work in the whole of the situation and could be trusted.

7

Embarking on an Unknown Journey:
The Responsible Use of Influence

Carol Zinn, SSJ

For the Traveler

Every time you leave home, another road takes you into a world you were never in.

New strangers on other paths await.
New places that have never seen you will startle a little at your entry.
Old places that know you well will pretend nothing changed since your last visit.

When you travel, you find yourself alone in a different way, more attentive now
to the self you bring along, your more subtle eye watching you abroad;
and how what meets you touches that part of the heart that lies low at home:

How you unexpectedly attune to the timbre in some voice, opening a conversation
you want to take in to where your longing has pressed hard enough inward,
on some unsaid dark, to create a crystal of insight you could not have known
you needed to illuminate your way.

When you travel, a new silence goes with you,
and if you listen, you will hear what your heart would love to say.

A journey can become a sacred thing: make sure, before you go,
to take the time to bless your going forth, to free your heart of ballast so that the
compass of your soul might direct you towards the territories

where you will discover your hidden life, and the urgencies that deserve to claim you.

May you travel in an awakened way, gathered wisely into your inner ground;
that you may not waste the invitations which wait along the way to transform you.

May you travel safely, arrive refreshed, and live your time to its fullest;
return home more enriched, and free to balance the gift of the days which call you.
-- John O'Donohue [1]

*J*ohn O'Donohue invites the reader to embrace the events and experiences in life as one would embark on a journey: as a traveler to a new and unknown place, yet at the same time, a surprisingly familiar and resonant place. Such a stance provides the space and pace for the necessary reflection, awareness, attentiveness, discipline, sustenance, discernment, receptivity, humility, vulnerability, courage, hope, and fidelity.

LCWR became a traveler in every aspect of John O'Donohue's poetic blessing. The journey from April 2012 to April 2015 placed LCWR in the public sphere, on a global stage, with a personal and institutional presence, for an unprecedented extended and intense experience of uncharted landscape. With this new light shining on the organization also came the realization that because LCWR was a respected organization, it had opportunities to use its influence in ways that could be helpful to others beyond itself.

LCWR knew that the question of exercising influence, that is, the capacity to have an effect on the character and/or development of behavior of someone or something, stood waiting at the doorstep of its soul. Carefully and consciously tending to the presence of this question became constitutive to the way in which LCWR navigated through the years of working on the mandate given to it by the Congregation for the Doctrine of the Faith (CDF).

The unknown places of this journey beckoned us to pay attention to myriad questions about how this navigation would unfold:

- How did the public nature of LCWR's conflict with the Vatican provide an opportunity for the conference to advocate for change on broader levels beyond LCWR?
- How did LCWR stay attuned to the hopes of the wider public for a transformed church and society, and allow those hopes to impact efforts to work with the Vatican?

- What kinds of decisions did LCWR face about its own responsible use of influence, and how were those decisions made?
- How did LCWR use its unique position *as an organization* (as opposed to an individual) under scrutiny to wisely advocate for change that would be beneficial to others beyond LCWR?
- What interior freedom did LCWR need to develop and how did it maintain and sustain the depth of such a foundational component for this journey?
- How did LCWR create the space for honest and genuine self-reflection as it traveled this journey so as to critique the inherent temptation to err in its responsible use of influence?

LCWR serves the elected leaders of women religious congregations in the United States. Its members represent about 80% of women religious living and serving in ministries of education, healthcare, social services, religious formation, and various aspects of the gospel message and Catholic social teaching.

As a national conference of women religious leaders, LCWR advocates not only for its own purposes but, because of the very nature of religious life, it also advocates for a range of issues and concerns related to contemporary gospel living. This work takes LCWR to the edge of the prophetic role of religious life itself: compassion and care for the most vulnerable and marginalized of society; commitment and concern for the human dignity of all; respect and reverence for the mutuality of relationships; recognition and responsibility for the furthering of the reign of God here and now.

Among women and men religious throughout the world, LCWR experiences a role of influence due to the privilege and blessing of its members' educational opportunities in theology, spirituality, and academia as well as the continuum of personal development through formation, leadership development, retreats, and spiritual direction. All this positioned LCWR as an organization in a place of influence through its presence, professionalism, publications, and programs that went far beyond the parameters of its members.

Thus, the scope of influence experienced by LCWR came into focus in a new way with the issuance of the mandate. And it called forth from us a serious discernment on how we would exercise a responsible use of our influence in a situation steeped in volatility.

This chapter explores LCWR's journey in the responsible use of influence through John O'Donohue's invitation to a traveler and the questions embraced during the experience with CDF. This exploration moves through the interplay between the words of John O'Donohue and the guiding direction of the questions.

Every time you leave home, another road takes you into a world you were never in.

How to exercise the responsible use of influence?

Almost immediately upon receiving the mandate from CDF in April 2012, it became clear that LCWR would be unable to move through this journey in its usual manner: privately and discreetly, while working to discern and implement a path forward. The response from the many publics came with rapid, incisive, and urgent messages, tones, and hopes. From the beginning it seemed LCWR would walk this journey in a spotlight it did not seek and within a global context it could not imagine.

From the beginning it seemed LCWR would walk this journey in a spotlight it did not seek and within a global context it could not imagine.

One of the questions that met LCWR at every turn remained pivotal throughout the journey: how to exercise the responsible use of influence as an organization of women, women religious, and women religious leaders? The realm of LCWR's influence became increasingly clear in the national and global response to the mandate.

In the media coverage, and in the range of emotions expressed by a cross-section of people, LCWR sensed a deeper resonance with the content of the mandate among many people. In the concerns raised by other national conferences of women and men religious beyond the United States, we recognized the scope of concern, fear, and betrayal in the minds and hearts of those who felt that their conference might be the next recipient of such a mandate. In the voices spoken by women's groups and justice groups we heard and felt their ache of discrimination, oppression, and inequality as they found themselves reflected in the content of the mandate. All of this found a home in our hearts, minds, ears, and souls as we began to discern our response.

New strangers on other paths await. New places that have never seen you will startle a little at your entry. Old places that know you well will pretend nothing changed since your last visit.

How did the public nature of LCWR's conflict with the Vatican provide an opportunity for the conference to advocate for change on broader levels beyond LCWR?

Acting within the context of the vision of Vatican Council II for 50 years, LCWR embraced the renewal of religious life with vigor, vitality, and vulnerability. The invitation presented in the Vatican Council II documents found a welcome in the minds and hearts of LCWR members in ways that offered transformative graces as the years of renewal opened threshold after threshold. One of those thresholds, the movement within the People of God towards a church whose fidelity to the gospel message would prompt significant and constitutive shifts in how the church perceives and lives out its mission in the world today, created a clarion call for changes across a spectrum of issues.

The intersection of religion and science, faith and reason, and the understanding of contemporary society became a graced precipice of consciousness within the renewal work.

The role of the laity, the relationship between the ordained and the laity, and the contribution of women in the church became a graced point of conversation in the renewal work. The celebration of the sacramental life of the church became a graced place of community through the renewal work. The intersection of religion and science, faith and reason, and the understanding of contemporary society became a graced precipice of consciousness within the renewal work. The gift of diversity in culture, race, gender, and belief and the place of the experience of God/Mystery in the institutional framework became a graced place of communion because of the renewal work. These ongoing renewal efforts towards a vision of a Vatican II church framed our every preparation for and participation in the multiple LCWR-CDF conversations.

These topics took on new meaning as the deeper understanding of the mandate unfolded. The role of the laity, the contribution of women, and where the space existed to discuss one's experience of God within the institutional framework of the Catholic Church informed some of the ways LCWR understood its responsible use of influence during this time. Since LCWR is a group of women religious leaders whose experience of God throughout the years of Vatican II renewal efforts seemed to contribute to the current conflict with the Vatican, the connection between the very profile of LCWR and the vision born at Vatican Council II could not be ignored.

Any conversation about the content of the mandate sat very close to some aspects of the role of the laity; the contribution of women; the exercise of leadership; the authenticity of one's experience of God, faith, and spirituality lived out in the contemporary world; and the safe and respectful places within the church where conversations about faith can happen without fear or judgment. The mandate flung open the door of thresholds in unexpected ways for all involved. Its sweeping accusations and prescriptive reform touched the heart of these thresholds for LCWR as well as for the wider church community and the even wider community of people here at home and around the world.

As LCWR discerned its way forward in April 2012, one of the first conversations we had with the LCWR national board revealed the inherent connections between the mandate and some of the aspects of the vision of Vatican II. From the very beginning of our work with the mandate, it was clear to us that this mandate did not exist in a vacuum and that while it was directed to LCWR, it was really about issues, perceptions, and realities that went beyond LCWR.

The extent to which the mandate resonated with people outside the LCWR organization compelled us to consider how we would chart a path forward. We realized that the components of the mandate were not only about LCWR as an organization or as a group of women religious leaders. Rather, there was a deeper conversation that yearned to emerge, a broader understanding of the core issues, and a profound movement of the Spirit prompting all of us to discernment and fidelity in new and challenging ways. The CDF mandate was about an adult, educated laity, in this case, a group of women religious, whose vision of a Vatican II church had guided their renewal, framed their discernment for more than 50 years, and claimed their fidelity.

We knew that as we moved forward with the mandate and its implementation, we would do so in the lens of the world's view. We knew that what we said or didn't say and how we acted or didn't act would have implications far beyond LCWR.

We came to understand that while the mandate was not the venue for advocating for broader changes beyond LCWR, it was, in fact a vehicle for the conversations about not only the broader changes beyond LCWR but the very real and painful reality of the need for these kinds of conversations. How LCWR chose to engage its responsible use of influence rose to the forefront of every deliberation and decision.

Once we individually and collectively understood these complexities, the careful, prayerful, thoughtful, and faithful response to the mandate ensued.

When you travel, you find yourself alone in a different way, more attentive now to the self you bring along, your more subtle eye watching you abroad; and how what meets you touches that part of the heart that lies low at home.

How did LCWR stay attuned to the hopes of the wider public for a transformed church and society, and allow those hopes to impact efforts to work with the Vatican?

Whenever we met to pray and discern the next step in the process of responding to the Vatican mandate, our prayer included the concerns, sufferings, and challenges of the larger world, country, and church. In this way we chose to keep before us the broader consequences of the absence of honest conversations, meaningful dialogue, and authentic desire for the common good. As the months and years moved on, the needs of the world continued to shape and fashion our own journey forward.

Hopes were expressed to LCWR from our own members, from the larger family of women religious, from the broader people of God, and from myriad justice groups. These hopes focused on many contemporary challenges. The care for our common home, Earth, had our attention. The unmet needs of the most vulnerable and marginalized women, men, and children around the world had our attention. The cries for inclusion over exclusion across seemingly impenetrable boundaries had our attention. The constant call of the gospel message of love and communion had our attention. The importance of relationships rooted in mutual respect, dignity, and compassion had our attention. These challenges remained present to us all of the time. And the consistent outpouring of support, affirmation, and solidarity from many voices and places buoyed us beyond our own limitations and inadequacies to continue to be faithful to the larger perspective within which something like this mandate could emerge.

As we journeyed, we sought out and listened to voices other than our own. We asked for help in keeping our eyes on the manner in which the mandate came into being. We relied on the depth of our own personal prayer as well as our communal prayer. Each time we met, either on the phone or in person, we began with a significant time of contemplative prayer. We shared an honest checking-in with one another to hear how this journey was impacting our lives and our ministries. And we had conversations about how the issues named in the mandate were indicative of larger contemporary issues within the church and society.

We found ourselves increasingly aware that we were alone in a different way and more attentive to the self we brought along on this journey. Fully cognizant that the mandate was about LCWR, we were consistently mindful that our hearts were touched by the sharpened sense within and among us that there was something quite profound at stake in this journey. We felt the hope of wanting our church to grow into the vision of Vatican II shared by so many. And we touched the deep ache experienced by so many in the absence of such a vision becoming reality.

Faithful to the mission of religious life as it responds to the needs of the times, our eyes, ears, minds, and hearts became acutely tuned to what was the work called forth in responding to the mandate. At the same time, we became just as aware of the work we

Whenever we met to pray and discern the next step in the process of responding to the Vatican mandate, our prayer included the concerns, sufferings, and challenges of the larger world, country, and church.

felt called to do by keeping the mandate within the broader perspective of the ecclesial and cultural environment in which the mandate was even able to see the light of day. This holy tension provided a necessary equilibrium for us and we came to both respect and rely on it.

How you unexpectedly attune to the timbre in some voice, opening a conversation you want to take in to where your longing had pressed hard enough inward, on some unsaid dark, to create a crystal of insight you could not have known you needed to illuminate your way.

What kinds of decisions did LCWR face about its own responsible use of influence, and how were those decisions made?

One of the most immediate decisions LCWR faced came to us on the very day we received the mandate from the CDF. We understood as we left that meeting on April 18, 2012 that we would return to the United States, gather the LCWR board members to share the mandate with them, seek their advice and direction, communicate with our organization's members, and prepare for engaging LCWR's response to the mandate at the August 2012 LCWR assembly of the members. LCWR is governed by its members so the response to the mandate would have to come from the members.

What we did not know until after we left the CDF office was that the mandate had been released to the website of the United States Conference of Catholic Bishops (USCCB) and it was already being read by our members as well as the media. We became immediately aware that our preferred mode of relating and responding, that is, in direct communication with our members and in a manner of reflection and thoughtful strategy was not possible.

How to respond to the needs of our members while we were in Rome? How to respond to the pressure from the media? How to manage our own desire to think this through in a way that provided ample time for study of the mandate and reflection on its implications, and created movement forward that came as a consequence of discernment and not reactionary impulse? How to respond to the inflammatory nature of the actions taken by the CDF and the USCCB? How to respond to the outrage that began to emerge? How to respond to the experience of being blind-sided by the issuance of the mandate and the way it was presented to us? And how to respond to the rising tide of emotions within each of us, among all of us, and beyond any of us? These questions rose from deep within us and remained with us throughout the entire time of working with the mandate.

> The decision to maintain a silent stance during the immediate time after the release of the mandate and a discreet stance throughout the journey of responding to the mandate came from a deep place of contemplation.

At the same time, we quickly realized that since LCWR was thrust onto a global stage with easy access to media, there was a serious point of integrity we had to engage. With the multiple opportunities before us to speak publicly, and the volatile atmosphere created by the public nature of the mandate, how would we think, discern, and act in a way that maintained our own integrity? How would we conduct ourselves during our remaining days in Rome? How would we encourage our members to engage the American media who were already hypersensitive to the tragedy of the sex-abuse scandal rocking the US Catholic Church? How would we advise our members to communicate with their members, associates, co-workers, and the public? How would we responsibly use the influence we did not seek but the potential influence we had?

What became clear while we were still in Rome was that without time to think, pray, and meet with the LCWR board to seriously and strategically explore and plan how to respond on all these levels, we would be less than who we were and who we were called to be. We decided that we would say nothing until we had the opportunity to gather the board members. We asked our members to honor the many processes by which we work together as LCWR and to give the board an opportunity to meet prior to the 2012 LCWR assembly before saying anything on the national, regional, or local levels -- at all.

This decision resonated with our members even though it was very difficult to maintain silence. We leaned heavily on the trust among us, the confidence we have in one another, and the innate awareness that this mandate was about more than LCWR. For six weeks LCWR said nothing publicly. For six weeks LCWR thought and prayed and sought counsel and studied the mandate and dealt with the range of emotions we were feeling.

After the board met in May 2012 and discerned a path forward, LCWR spent the months of June and July preparing its members for the August assembly. This plan included regional meetings with our members to help process the range of real and valid emotions and discern how to best move forward. The plan also included continuing to seek counsel about the content and conditions of the mandate. And it provided time to design a process by which more than 900 women religious leaders could engage the experience of the mandate at the assembly and over the course of four days come to some consensus about how to move forward.

For the second time since April, LCWR discerned to maintain silence in the public sphere. We did so because we knew that what we said, when we said it, how we said it, and to whom we said it would either add or detract from the essential work of the mandate. It is also important to note that LCWR and the archbishop delegate shared an acute awareness of the role of the media in this situation. And for that reason, we made the mutual commitment we would not speak to each other through the media nor would we use the media to speak about each other. That commitment held throughout this entire process and still holds today.

The decision to maintain a silent stance during the immediate time after the release of the mandate and a discreet stance throughout the journey of responding to the mandate came from a deep place of contemplation. It was not an easy decision at any point along the way. The temptation to exercise an influence we knew we had was presented to us many times during the three-year journey.

The responsible use of our influence was ever before us because we knew that the content of the mandate touched the lives of many other people. We were not the only ones who felt unheard or dismissed, had been identified as being unfaithful to church teaching, or were struggling to find a safe place where conversations about our faith could happen with respect for diversity and genuine search for meaning. We were not the only ones who held a deep hope in the vision of a Vatican II church and world.

When you travel, a new silence goes with you, and if you listen, you will hear what your heart would love to say.

How did LCWR use its unique position as an organization under scrutiny (as opposed to an individual) to wisely advocate for change that would be beneficial to others beyond LCWR?

As we moved through the years of reflection and discernment, we grew in our realization of the capacity we had to influence the conversations between LCWR and the CDF and with the archbishop delegate. We knew that the deeper levels of conversation drew everyone involved into questions of faith, authority, relationship, church teachings, pastoral practices, identity, and community.

Moving into the depth of the relationship was critical to the process. We desired to hear and speak what our hearts would love to say. We yearned to share in the mutuality of adult believers, faithful disciples of Jesus, and graced daughters of the church. We began to hear a new silence speak to us, a silence that beckoned a new courage. And we leaned into that silence and courage not for ourselves only but for a hurting world, a wounded church, a fragile nation, and a broken sense of oneness and communion.

We chose to act in a way that would not further polarize any of the persons involved or the topics discussed. This choice called forth our most mature selves and our best selves. It demanded a discipline born of discernment, a gentleness born of grace, and a solidarity born of spaciousness.

Each time we met among ourselves or with the archbishop delegate or CDF, we remained steadfast in respectfully posing the question at the heart of the mandate: in what way(s) are we unfaithful? This haunting question carved a deep space within us and it allowed us to keep focused on the desire to engage in honest dialogue based on mutual respect.

Posing this question gave us a way to remain painfully aware of the fact that countless individuals had gone before us in this same manner of inquisition. We recalled people we knew who had sat in the same chairs we sat in when we met at the CDF offices and some of those people heard similar things said about their fidelity and integrity. This memory helped our awareness that the LCWR mandate was delivered to an organization and so an organization needed to respond as an organization and not as a group of individuals. We chose to remain focused on the public, organizational nature of the mandate while responding in personal, communal ways. This stance kept our responsible use of influence ever before us.

A journey can become a sacred thing; make sure before you go, to take the time to bless your going forth, to free your heart of ballast so that the compass of your soul might direct you towards the territories where you will discover your hidden life, and the urgencies that deserve to claim you.

What interior freedom did LCWR need to develop and how did it maintain and sustain the depth of such a foundational component for this journey?

We consistently made the time for communal prayer and we trusted that each of us tended to her own personal prayer as well her own inner work of emotional maturity, healthy inter-personal relationship skills, and clarity of thought and purpose. We were also sensitive to the presence of "agendas" when we met. We kept the purity of intention foremost in our conversations and deliberations.

Mindful that it was easy for any one of us to take a deep dive into arrogance, righteousness, or myopic perspective, we gave one another permission to monitor the movement of graces received and graces refused among us.

Mindful that it was easy for any one of us to take a deep dive into arrogance, righteousness, or myopic perspective, we gave one another permission to monitor the movement of graces received and graces refused among us. This proved invaluable to our communal discernment and collective leadership.

The compass of our soul directed us to the places within us where we did discover our hidden life, that is, the depth of our commitment to the Gospel and to religious life. This, in turn, brought us face-to-face with the urgencies that deserved to claim us: fidelity, integrity, honesty, compassion, deep listening, vulnerability, humility, hope, and love as the ingredients for all human relationships. And human relationships are the places where we encounter God. Our love for the Gospel, religious life, the people of God and all creation, and our desire to create a space in which mutual dialogue might take place called us onward at every turn in the journey.

Our commitment to a responsible use of influence served as guardian and guide as we carefully and prayerfully considered every step along the way.

How we might contribute to the creation of adult relationships within the church and the bridging of broken relationships served as subtext to every conversation and action.

May you travel in an awakened way, gathered wisely into your inner ground; that you may not waste the invitations which wait along the way to transform you. May you travel safely, arrive refreshed, and live your time to its fullest; return home more enriched, and free to balance the gift of the days which call you.

Our hope rests in the wisdom gleaned through LCWR's experience as a traveler open to the journey and receptive to the blessings along the way. This stance offered LCWR the opportunity to engage this moment in its history from a depth of prayer, reflection, discernment, contemplation, collaboration, and courage. As with all travelers, there is a perspective that can only be realized after the journey ends. While we might not have used John O'Donohue's words at the onset of the CDF journey, we resonate with his words now and, in retrospect, at many points along the way of the journey.

Our hope compels us to believe:

- That traveling safely implies traveling together.
- That arriving refreshed suggests attending to how you discern and navigate each moment of the journey.
- That living your time to its fullest demands thoughtful attention and strategic planning all along the way.
- That returning home more enriched invites a depth of understanding and focus on the most important elements of the journey.
- And that being free to balance the gift of the days which call you remains the most meaningful, holy and whole aim of all, however long the night.

Endnote

1. "For the Traveler," from *To Bless the Space Between Us: A Book of Blessings* by John O'Donohue, copyright © 2008 by John O'Donohue. Used by permission of Doubleday, an imprint of the Knopf Doubleday Publishing Group, a division of Penguin Random House LLC. All rights reserved.

For Reflection and Dialogue

1. As you consider your personal/organization's use of influence, how would you describe it? How is it determined? Where is it exercised and by whom? Can you recall a time when the outcome of your use of influence furthered your intended goal? Why do you think the outcome furthered the intended goal? Can you recall a time when the outcome of your use of influence failed to further the intended goal? Why do you think the outcome failed to further the intended goal? What was your learning in each situation?

2. Influence unfolds in human interactions. A smile or frown, a nod of recognition or a negation of another's presence, a word of affirmation or a sneer of affront all have the capacity to influence another. What kind of careful attention do you/your organization give to the use of your influence? How do you craft the exercise of your influence?

3. In situations of conflict, oftentimes it is the more subtle use of influence that carries more weight. This is referred to as "soft influence." How might "soft influence" be determined and exercised in you/your organization? What might this "soft influence" look like in a particular situation? Can you create a plan for this kind of influence? What would you/your organization have to learn? Practice?

As with all travelers, there is a perspective that can only be realized after the journey ends.

8

The Power of Secrecy and Perceptions

Sharon Holland, IHM

In Douglas Wood's charming tale, Old Turtle,[1] all of the creatures begin to proclaim the nature of God -- from their own perspective.

"She is a great tree...always growing and giving" the willow murmured, but the island countered, "You are wrong...God is separate and apart."

"She is a hunter," roared the lion.

"God is gentle," chirped the robin.

"He is powerful," growled the bear.

Then came the startling sound of Old Turtle's voice: "Stop!" Into the silence, Old Turtle spoke affirmation of all of the images. No one image was adequate. "God is all that we dream of, and all that we seek," said Old Turtle, "all that we come from and all that we can find. God IS."

In the tale, no creature's image of God was wrong. All spoke from their own perspective, from "where they stood." Each had the potential to grow and enjoy a fuller view. We are not told how long it took the creatures to stand in new places and change perspective. Humanity had not yet appeared on the scene.

As in the story, fragmented bits of truth characterized the early stages of the doctrinal assessment of the Leadership Conference of Women Religious (LCWR) by the Congregation for the Doctrine of the Faith (CDF). Sisters frequently asked, "Where is this coming from?" "Why is this happening?" "Is this about doctrine or docility?"

As a staff member of the Vatican's Congregation for Institutes of Consecrated Life and Societies of Apostolic Life (CICLSAL) from 1988 to 2009, I was present for many of LCWR's annual visits to that dicastery. I had witnessed the efforts of successive members of the LCWR presidency to understand or explain various concerns raised by officials. It was not always immediately evident that those efforts had failed, but the same issues often recurred the next year: departure from traditional ministries, different living patterns, the drop in the number of vocations.

In retrospect, one can wonder if there was ever an effort to pass on to those who complained to the dicastery about LCWR, the explanations they had received. LCWR was not speaking with the accusers and could not tell if the officials were convinced by their responses.

After the mandate was issued, and efforts to confront it were underway at LCWR, I was haunted by memories from my last year in Rome. There were echoes of grievances against US women religious, specifically LCWR. I recall registering that, from my point of view, some were quite out of date while others were exaggerated or simply untrue. The charges were, at least, the perceptions of prelates who were convinced of our disloyalty, disrespect, or error.

There had been mention, on occasion, of a visitation to all women religious in the United States, but it had seemed to me an impossible task. I was angered by my sense of helplessness to do anything after it was announced.

Before I left the dicastery, two processes had been set in motion in quick succession: the apostolic visitation of all US apostolic women religious and the doctrinal assessment of LCWR. The structure of the Roman Curia required two distinct actions according to competencies: CICLSAL and CDF. CICLSAL oversees the life and ministry of religious throughout the world; CDF examines and judges the authenticity of theological statements and writings which have been questioned.

I learned of the actual launching of each of these through phone calls from the LCWR national offices in Maryland, even though the initiatives emanated from an office just down the hall. This certainly was another frustrating lack of transparency. The visitation was publicly launched in 2009 and was carried forward with extensive communication from the visitor to all congregational leaders regarding personnel and processes.

The doctrinal assessment was also announced to LCWR officials in 2009. Representatives of CDF did their research in LCWR files, but its results were made known only when the doctrinal assessment and mandate were published by CDF in April 2012.

> The question continually arises: When does confidentiality (or secrecy) provide necessary protection, and when does it protect some at the expense of others?

The LCWR presidency received that document and heard it read to them at their regular April 2012 meeting with CDF; they were given to understand that the text would not be made public immediately. Someone didn't know about that promise, or didn't think it prudent. The document appeared on the public side of the USCCB website almost before the LCWR officers left the meeting. Tensions mounted. In the absence of information, religious began to speculate about who was behind the assessment. Individuals, groups, and events were named as possibly providing the impetus for the assessment. Some of these seemed plausible; some were probably untrue.

The presidency was left with the difficult job of "damage control." Between April 2012 and the August assembly, reactions, questions, and speculations grew. "Who was behind this?" "Why was it happening"? "Why now?" "Why hadn't we been informed?" Fear, hurt, and anger were evident. For people committed to a great deal of transparency, the whole matter was profoundly disturbing.

In the chandeliered ballroom of the convention hotel hosting the 2012 assembly, members prayed and discerned about a right path forward. In prayer and silence the presence of the Spirit was palpable. In that charged atmosphere, the assembled membership found the strength to take the next step forward in peace, maintaining its integrity.

The research carried out by CDF-appointed officials (2009-2012) placed in question our members' fundamental ecclesial fidelity. Religious who had studied and worked to implement all of the documents of Vatican Council II felt misjudged and offended. They had taken up the challenge of renewal issued in *Perfectae caritatis* (the Council's document on the renewal of religious life) with the utmost seriousness; there was hurt and anger. Elderly religious were deeply troubled. Those who had lived in fidelity for decades now asked if they had done something wrong.

In retrospect, and aware of the experience of both the visitation and the assessment, we can again reflect on the effects of secrecy or, in today's language, a lack of transparency.

The church itself has been deeply disturbed by the question of secrecy in recent years. What was viewed in past decades as appropriate confidentiality, protecting the reputation of clerics and of the church, began to be seen as a dangerous and unhealthy secrecy. The grave injustice of protecting an adult while leaving a child unprotected had begun to loom large.

Was there a question of confidentiality in the processes surrounding LCWR? In the early reports of complaints received by CICLSAL, no names of accusers were revealed to LCWR, nor were they asked for. The request from LCWR was only that if bishops had complaints, they would bring them directly to the religious.

The question continually arises: When does confidentiality (or secrecy) provide necessary protection, and when does it protect some at the expense of others?

We know of the secrecy practiced in the past which was a grave injustice, though not then understood as such. Families with mentally or physically challenged children kept them hidden, out of the sight of visitors. They were not spoken of; ignorance, a sense of shame, and the absence of modern medical and psychological help led parents of these children to keep them, often literally, hidden in the dark. Likewise, children today are the victims when they are taught never to speak of addictive behavior and abuse experienced in their homes.

In contrast, other persons have been secretly hidden in darkness to save them. This secrecy saved many from the anti-Jewish pogroms or other modes of ethnic "cleansing." Heroism saved lives and wove lifelong bonds of friendship and gratitude.

Obviously, secrecy has many faces. Children love secrets, and they love to whisper them to a friend. There can be great fun in a surprise birthday or anniversary party. But what if a secret communication is not true? What if people are accused, but know nothing of a high-level communication about them?

Successive LCWR presidents had urged that prelates who complained about a specific woman religious be asked to contact the religious directly so that there might be dialogue about the issues. Efforts by LCWR over the years to explain to Vatican officials community-living patterns, and the relationship between new ministries and an institute's charism which would have clarified some of the complaints apparently had not been effective.

By the time CDF was preparing the document presenting their assessment (doctrinal findings), along with the mandate (the corrections to be made), they were aware that the Final Report of the Apostolic Visitation had been submitted to the Holy See through CICLSAL, (December 2011). In retrospect, reading both documents, one can see that the basically positive Visitation Report, made public in December 2014, must have presented challenges to those responsible for the mandate. The findings in the report did not reflect the negativity of the assessment.

A study of the doctrinal assessment together with the mandate seems to present diverse perspectives about the doctrinal positions held by American women religious (in this context, members of LCWR). The first part of the 2012 document was the result of the assessment which had been initiated in 2009. The second part, the mandate, indicated the necessary corrections to be made under the direction of the bishops assigned to oversee the process. Some of the issues in the assessment did not appear in the mandate for further action.

The introduction to the assessment used the words with which Pope John Paul II praised American religious in his 1987 address in San Francisco. "I rejoice because of your deep love of the Church and your generous service to God's people." The document then identified a perception that LCWR's sense of the Christological center of religious life and its lively sense of church were lessening. The goal was to assist LCWR in implementing an ecclesiology of communion.

The CDF document expressed concern over distorted notions of church, questionable stances on women's ordination and homosexuality, and stances of radical feminism which threatened, among other things, a right theology of God. Undoubtedly, some prelates honestly believed we were off track on certain doctrinal matters; some simply were convinced that we were disrespectful of ecclesiastical authority. Some bishops would simply assume that what was reported by CDF was true, even if they had not personally experienced it. Efforts to discuss or respond to various perceptions prior to the public phase of the process seemed to be of no avail. This too gave rise to the question of why the explanations were of no avail.

A moment of critical insight came during a 2014 meeting between LCWR and CDF before the conclusion of the mandate. During the discussion, a CDF official expressed regret that certain perceptions had become "institutionalized." Something which perhaps should have been obvious, suddenly was made clear to me when it was named. Understandings, stereotypes, and perceptions were passed on and on, without critique. For example, "American religious women are disrespectful toward church authority, unfaithful to basic religious practices, don't live in community, don't participate in Eucharist ...." The Apostolic Visitation Report had dismissed this generalized, negative image, while encouraging positive attention to the various aspects of religious life.

In retrospect, we can understand that the research done using LCWR files could not produce proof of LCWR doctrinal deviations. The accusations, we can see more clearly now, were based on institutionalized perceptions, which closer examination did not substantiate. What an individual said, even in passing, did not constitute a public stance of the conference, nor was it perpetuated in time.

Understanding such institutionalized perceptions assists us in realizing the complexity of what we might call a cultural chasm.

It must be acknowledged. however, that this truth cuts both ways. If there were Vatican officials perpetuating negative perceptions about US religious, there were also religious reciting another litany: "Bishops are authoritarian, they distrust women, they just want docility." Individual experiences were allowed to cast a shadow on all.

Understanding such institutionalized perceptions assists us in realizing the complexity of what we might call a cultural chasm. This is much deeper than languages spoken. This has to do with "where we stand" while viewing realities. Like the friends of Old Turtle we see from where we are, rarely aware that things can also be viewed from a different, but not necessarily wrong, perspective. Until such differences can be brought to awareness, the "other" seems not only "foreign" but wrong.

The understanding of authority in the church is a critical case in point. This issue intersects with the roles of men and of women, cleric and lay, educated or illiterate, formed by Vatican II or not. What needed to be brought to consciousness in our situation was the historical, cultural context which gave rise to ideas, practices, and perceptions. We had all failed to sufficiently examine our institutionalized perceptions of each other.

One of my favorite examples of awareness of cultural gaps came during Pope John Paul II's visit in San Francisco. While I don't have the exact words, this insight came from the woman, a wife and mother, who addressed the pope on behalf of the laity. In essence, she said: "Holy Father, please understand that when we ask questions we are not rebelling against the church. We have been educated to ask questions and think critically. We want to understand."[2]

> ... we all see from our own perspective. That does not produce full truth, but one legitimate dimension of the truth.

For me, this seemed to illustrate the meaning of a "cultural chasm." There was a mentality of an American woman of the 20th century, devoted to the church. For her, however, this also meant the desire, the need to learn and to understand church teachings which affected her life and that of her family. One cultural approach could have understood this as arrogant and a lack of docility to the church and its teachings. A different cultural perception saw it as a normal and necessary way of deepening and living an adult faith.

However, as the Old Turtle's wisdom indicates, we all see from our own perspective. That does not produce full truth, but one legitimate dimension of the truth. These words remind us of Pope Paul VI's insights regarding dialogue. All participants must recognize that they have only a part of the truth.

A part of one's reality resides in the mind and can be reflected on. Another essential part resides in the heart, and unless brought to the level of consciousness it will not change, but will color rational reflection. Vatican II's Decree on Bishops, *Christus Dominus*, states that the desired close collaboration between bishops and religious "will depend mainly on a supernatural attitude of heart and mind grounded on charity" (n. 35.5).

A part of our difficulty seems to be that we are not even aware of the chasm or, perhaps, that we are seeing only our own perceived reality. We know our truth and do not understand that it is not what is perceived by the other. We accept what we perceive of the other as fact, without considering if that is the other's perception as well. In the last analysis, we may say that no one is really seeing or hearing. Or we are not aware that the other sees things differently than we do. We can ask if anyone is deeply listening.

LCWR had long been seeking to enter into all processes and discussions in an attitude and atmosphere of contemplation, that is, of a deeper, quieter reflection. This was an effort by individual members, and by the assembly when together. Sinking deeper into a question offered new insights. This served us well in trying to deal with the doctrinal assessment, but not without struggle. Sometimes such a conflict cannot be resolved by the parties themselves.

This story of secrecy and institutionalized perceptions cannot be told without speaking of the role of Archbishop J. Peter Sartain of Seattle, who was appointed to journey with us. He, with his assistants, was to oversee the fulfillment of the mandate. He broke the pattern of institutionalized perceptions by asking for resources from LCWR to help him understand how LCWR congregations had gone about the renewal called for by Vatican Council II. This, we may add, also broke through our institutionalized perceptions of how a delegate of CDF would proceed.

The national office prepared executive summaries of important books, delivered them, and discussed them with the archbishop. He did not assume he knew us well; he did not assume he had all of the necessary information in the assessment. He took his role seriously and was trying to understand, from our vantage point. Throughout the process he worked tirelessly to translate understanding between CDF and LCWR. His great personal integrity made it possible for him to truly mediate, patiently helping CDF officials and LCWR officials understand what was happening between them.

Month by month we began to see ourselves and those accusing us more clearly. We also began to perceive more clearly not only the long-time perceptions, but the complexity of publicly unraveling the tangled process. In any such process, listening is essential. Deep listening to what another is saying is crucial and, beyond the words, hearing what further meaning may be there.

We slowly realized that CDF personnel wanted to find a way to conclude the process as much as we did. We needed to show that the concerns of the mandate had actually been addressed. It was no longer useful for us to insist that there had never been cause for a mandate in the first place.

On April 16, 2015, the "Joint Final Report" was issued. Those who are familiar with procedures of the Roman Curia will recognize that the raesults of a CDF study of the doctrinal stances of an individual or group, normally end with a statement from the dicastery. This process ended with a joint report.

The opening of the joint report states: "From the beginning, our extensive conversations were marked by a spirit of prayer, love for the Church, mutual respect and cooperation." It then sets forth "the manner in which the implementation of the Mandate has been accomplished." It is signed by the three bishop delegates, the three members of the LCWR presidency, and the LCWR executive director.

Whatever the merits of the original mandate, perhaps we could not have begun to deinstitutionalize the perceptions and bridge the cultural chasms without the religious and episcopal team which carried it through.

We can recognize now that unnecessary secrecy and institutionalized perceptions were impacting our lives. Was the secrecy a serious problem? Perhaps not, but the lack of openness and transparency, so emphasized in US culture, aggravated distrust and fear. We found it difficult to trust a process which was begun secretly. At the beginning it left in place the perceptions institutionalized in our minds and in those of the persons investigating us.

We can also see from this distance in years rich with reflection that the Holy Spirit was powerfully present. In a nation and a world so torn by hate, war, and divisions such a story can seem small. And yet, no life is small and every lesson learned has value for the future.

As Wood's story continues, Old Turtle relates that a strange and wonderful new family of beings would come. They would be "a message of love from God to earth, and a prayer from the earth back to God." And the people came.

But later, the people forgot. They "could not remember who they were, or where God was" and they were hurting one another and the earth.

After "a long, lonesome and scary time the people listened, and began to hear... And to see God in one another and in the beauty of all the Earth."

"And Old Turtle smiled. And so did God."

For Reflection and Dialogue

1. When have you experienced having your perspective on an issue broadened or changed by deeply listening to other persons?

2. Have you ever felt judged according to an "institutionalized perception"? Have you allowed an individual negative experience to cast a shadow over a whole category of persons?

3. What experiences or relationships have helped you bridge a "cultural chasm" in the church, society, or in an organization?

Endnotes

1. From *Old Turtle* by Douglas Wood. Scholastic Inc./Scholastic Press. Copyright © 1992 by Douglas Wood. Reprinted by permission.

2. Roberto Suro, "The Papal Visit: Pope Hears Woman's Plea to Give Laity Larger Voice." *New York Times,* September 19, 1987.

9

A Spiritual Journey:
What We Learned About Humility

Mary Hughes, OP

Humility is to be still
under the weathers of God's will.
It is to have no hurt surprise
when morning's ruddy promise dies,
when wind and drought destroy, or sweet
spring rains apostatize in sleet,
or when the mind and month remark
a superfluity of dark.
It is to have no troubled care for human weathers anywhere.
And yet it is to take the good
with the warm hand of gratitude.
Humility is to have a place
Deep in the secret of God's face
where one can know, past all surmise
that God's great will alone is wise,
where one is loved, where one can trust
a strength not circumscribed by dust.
It is to have a place to hide
when all is hurricane outside.
-- Sister Miriam of the Holy Spirit, OCD (Jessica Powers)

*A*mong the gifts Jessica Powers offered to our world is this poem entitled "Humility." This Carmelite woman's contemplative reflection moves us quickly beneath any superficial understandings and invites us into a deeper wellspring of spiritual wisdom.

Two separate journeys were being undertaken by LCWR members when the efforts to respond to concerns on the part of some Catholic Church officials came crashing down in the form of the mandate from the Congregation for the Doctrine of the Faith (CDF). In order to craft responses and develop plans of action there was the journey of study, analysis, and intellectual critique to lay bare both truth and untruth. Many fine scholars supported the LCWR members with this analysis and in the unpeeling of issues. Each sister brought to the table her finest abilities and the significance of the mandate strengthened our resolve to work as one.

The parallel journey was the spiritual journey that each woman underwent. There are so many ways in which one might respond to trauma. The feelings of shock, bewilderment, betrayal, anger, and even hopelessness were all among them. For each sister directly and indirectly involved, the timeline might vary but the feelings were intense whenever they surfaced. Yet these feelings, although acutely experienced, would not necessarily carry us through all that needed to be done while still leading a membership-driven organization. We tried to articulate the spiritual dimension that God was asking us to embrace at this moment in time. It did not take long for humility to be identified as a hallmark of our efforts. Humility became both the working mode and the spiritual gift. The journeys became very much intertwined and each tapped into deep aspects of our lives.

Humility

*H*umility is a virtue that can be difficult to describe. It is often explained by what it is not. Humility is not groveling nor is it having a subservient attitude nor is it denial of the gifts one has been given. It does include a profound awareness of the author and giver of the personal and collective gifts we possess. Gifts are intended, one might even say mandated, for use. Matthew 5:15 reminds us the light is not to be hidden under the lampstand. The passage in Luke 12:48 states clearly that when one has been given a great deal, much will be asked.

Humility comes with the invitation to be truthful about one's faults and shortcomings. It is the invitation to stand naked before a mirror and honestly assess one's moments of pride, of brashness, of failures, or of any misuse of gifts. It is an examen that is best conducted while seeking God's grace and mercy so that we might, at least for a few moments, see ourselves as God sees us.

The Catechism of the Catholic Church speaks of humility, specifically as it was manifested by Mary, in the acceptance of her invitation to be the Mother of God. The text also speaks of humility as lived out in the mission and crucifixion of Jesus (559, 724). It speaks of the "humility of his flesh" (724) and "humility that bears witness to the truth" (559). These examples serve to remind us that even one who leads a life of goodness and virtue is not guaranteed an absence of suffering.

> *It is to have no surprise*
> *when morning's ruddy promise dies,*
> *when wind and drought destroy, or sweet*
> *spring rains apostatize in sleet,*
> *or when the mind and month remark*
> *a superfluity of dark.*

Acting out of humility caused us to ask many questions and the self-imposed weeks of prayer and refraining from public comment after we received the mandate gave us the reflective time to grapple with the answers that emerged. After all, "Humility is to be still under the weathers of God's will."

Did we do something wrong? Did we fail to communicate? What was God's will? Such questions were often followed by wishes of "If only," "Did they realize?" Were we holding assumptions that did not hold up under the test of time? All of these assumptions needed to be examined, held to the light, and either acknowledged or dispelled.

If humility was to be a way through the conversations and negotiations, we would need to guard against arrogance, righteousness, or pretense. We would proceed with a commitment to truth, respect for all persons who might be in dialogue with us, and confidence in God's companionship on this difficult journey.

Cultural Diversity and Assumptions

Each of us is formed and shaped by the cultures within which we have grown up and lived. There are the cultures of ethnic origin, race, gender, language, religious denomination, and even age. These are large categories and easily recognizable. Interwoven with these large categories are the myriad of sub-cultures that contribute to shaping us into the person we have become thus far. For instance, educational institutions help to shape our patterns of reading, research, and ability to locate information on one's own. Such membership can also contribute to perceptions of privilege. Socioeconomic status also carries with it cultural norms. Persons who come from a high socioeconomic stratum have resources affording the ability to choose private education, to dress well, to spend time with persons within the same stratum, and to travel and recreate in wonderful if not exotic ways. Persons who are born into a lower level of economic means have completely different realities. Family, the primary container shaping one's being, possesses traditions involving food, ways of honoring family members, patterns of relationship, as well as concepts of authority.

> If humility was to be a way through the conversations and negotiations, we would need to guard against arrogance, righteousness, or pretense.

Each of these realities are merely different and contribute to the wonderful diversity that is humankind. The inherent danger is that one can come to believe that one's way of being is the only way, the best way, or the right way. Although the members of CDF and Catholic sisters all belong to the same church, they often have culturally diverse experiences. Such diversity can enrich the church immeasurably. However, such diverse experiences also hold the potential for conflict and misunderstanding.

There are any number of assumptions one can unconsciously carry, but there are probably three that were particularly operative during not only the days after the reception of the mandate, but also in the months and even years that preceded its issuance. Assumptions were carried by sisters belonging to LCWR as well as by the staff of the CDF office.

- As well-educated persons working on behalf of the church, we likely exercise our responsibilities in much the same way.

- Although the Catholic Church is comprised of people from a diversity of countries and cultures, we understand, practice, and celebrate our faith in the same ways.
- Although there are multiple forms of religious life, there is really one "best" way to live it.

To address the first assumption, religious congregations in the United States have grown up in a country that prizes individualism and democracy. Both of these qualities have their shadow or darker side. Although it has been said that religious life is countercultural, one must acknowledge that these cultural norms have seeped into the very bones of US sisters. In our earliest history, whether the religious community developed within the country or sisters came as missionaries, sisters were drawn to respond to the many needs of God's people. As they founded new missions, meager communication systems did not always allow for seeking approval from elected superiors in other countries or regions. After Vatican II, sisters studied their founding charisms and developed broader and more inclusive forms of governance. There is a long history of adaptations.

Annually, the presidency of LCWR and the executive director went to the Vatican with a list of pre-scheduled visits to various offices whose work might intersect with that of the many religious congregations in the United States. For instance, LCWR always made a request to visit the office dealing with Institutes of Consecrated Life and Societies of Apostolic Life. This was a particular office where one might seek fruitful dialogue about the challenges facing religious life in regions other than our own.

In addition to this very important visit, there were visits to offices whose primary work was dedicated to justice and peace, immigrants, evangelization, inter-religious dialogue, or the family. This is a sample listing rather than an exhaustive one. Prior to each annual visit there was a request to visit the Congregation for the Doctrine of the Faith. There was often a request to visit the Secretary of State. There was, most often, a request to attend the liturgy celebrated by the Holy Father if he were in town at that time.

This travel and the various visits were completely paid for by the conference in the belief that it is very important to keep our ties with the larger church clear and strong. We went to Rome in the company of the Conference of Major Superiors of Men (CMSM). We visited some offices together but visited others individually. During each visit, the conference representatives were prepared with some initial remarks highlighting the most recent work of the conference. The visits were generally about an hour in length and there was care given to leaving time for both questions and discussion.

Like all plans put on paper, there were pieces of the plan that worked and there were other pieces that failed to meet expectations. There were years that an individual office did not respond to the request or there was a last-minute change. While there is warmth and dialogue in most offices at this moment in time, it was not always so. There were times when LCWR gave its reports and there were no questions nor was there an invitation to further elaboration on any of the topics. There were, at times, statements of judgment made by the Vatican office without supporting examples being articulated.

It was humbling to experience the consequences of our lack of awareness.

The LCWR women offering the oral reports held the expectation or assumption that questions would be the entrée to rich dialogue. If there were no questions, there was the assumption that all was clear. Sharon Holland, IHM analyzed the reality well in her 2015 LCWR presidential address entitled "Attitudes of Heart and Mind." While LCWR's hope for these Vatican meetings was for dialogue, sometimes the meetings were actually parallel conversations, both verbal and non-verbal. Each party to the conversation left with their personal perceptions. The LCWR report, offered to elucidate, may not have been "heard" at all. The questions most in need of answering might not have been asked. Whatever rumors or reports about LCWR that precipitated suspicion might not have been articulated. It was the foundation for a perfect storm.

While there was likely cultural blindness in multiple places, we must acknowledge we from LCWR may have carried the assumption that our ways of governance and inclusion were so valuable to us that those in the Vatican would have easily understood them. Dialogue has revealed to us that this is not necessarily so. While our ways of self-governance as an organization are most often respected, they have not necessarily been the catalyst for change on the part of other offices or organizations. Just as we might be tempted to identify potential shortfalls in other, less democratic forms of leadership, shortfalls about our leadership modes were also being identified. We knew this at some level. It was humbling to experience the consequences of our lack of awareness.

The second assumption, implying that cultures come together somewhat magically under the umbrella of church membership, was one that played an important part in the miscues. Although the Vatican is situated in Rome, the offices are populated by persons who have homes of origin in other parts of the world. Each ethnic culture has ways of praying that are precious to its people. There are differing concepts of personal space, of time, and of how to address matters of delicacy. At times there are gender expectations about who does the speaking and how. During the years when the mandate was operative, we began with a pope who was from Bavaria and was succeeded by a pontiff who spent almost all his life in Argentina. Each person comes fully immersed in the rich Catholic heritage that is particular to his or her origins. Add to this, the complex reality of LCWR.

> Once again our American spirit, seeking to make a place for the voice of all, may have assumed that the value of what we do is always clear.

LCWR is not a governance body. It is a membership organization that seeks to assist its members, elected leaders in their respective congregations, in the ministry entrusted to them. In this effort to support, the conference walks a fine line. It can offer advice and connect members with persons of expertise in a variety of areas. It cannot tell a member congregation what it can or cannot do. If a member of a religious congregation acts in a way that draws public attention to her wisdom or lack of it, it is not the role of the conference to intervene or to tell the individual community what it should do.

This kind of model differs from that under which most of the church operates. The pope possesses the authority of leadership. There are layers of persons who support the governance of the church and its members. If an ordained clergy person acts or speaks against the prevailing norms, there is usually quick and speedy action.

One might wonder if those in the Vatican with whom LCWR met over the years expected conference leaders to report on particular events that occurred in a specific religious institute. Of interest might have been how the event was handled and what disciplinary action, if any, was exercised. However, such matters would never be in any LCWR report because it is not the domain of the conference to address such issues.

Another concern expressed by CDF to LCWR in the mandate was that of the role of speakers at LCWR assemblies. Because the conference seeks to be a support to elected leaders, speakers are often selected because of their ability to speak to a dimension of leadership. The elected leaders of religious congregations are, by and large, a highly educated group of women. Among them are theologians, educators, former college and hospital presidents, social workers, scientists, and leaders in a variety of professions. While there have been speakers who addressed conference members on scripture, Vatican II, and trends in religious life, there is no consistent practice suggesting members will be further educated in teachings of the church at a conference. Most, if not all, have access to Catholic colleges and universities offering stimulating and informative lectures on church matters. Rather than duplicate such offerings, the conference seeks speakers who will stretch understanding of subjects such as the unfolding universe, of grieving and resurrection theology, and of institutional racism.

It should be noted, there is not always uniform agreement among the LCWR members on any speaker. Table conversations are lively and one can expect disagreement as well as agreement on any number of topics. Speakers are not always of our faith but there is openness to hearing their truth and to the stretching that better equips leaders to meet the complex challenges of the women we serve and the people of God we have come to love. LCWR is not a theological conference. It is a conference of and for leaders.

This kind of latitude is not a hallmark of conferences of Catholic bishops nor of some other conferences of religious, nor is it always seen as a value. Once again our American spirit, seeking to make a place for the voice of all, may have assumed that the value of what we do is always clear.

The third assumption might be that there is a single best way to live religious life. Over the centuries the church has been blessed with a growing number of forms of religious life. Among these are hermits, monastics, itinerants, apostolic communities, as well as a myriad of newer communities. These are manifestations of God's imagination and spirit. Some congregations embrace a more traditional form of religious life and dress. Others have realized their founders and foundresses were clothed in the contemporary garb of the time and have done the same. Each congregation brings the spirit and gift of its charism and often each might reach people of God not reached by another. One might certainly have preferences but to legislate on the basis of preference is to stifle the work of the Holy Spirit. The mandate, issued to a particular cohort of apostolic women religious in the United States, was experienced as an assault on our very way of life.

The severity and heavy-handedness of the mandate came from the very church to which we had given our lives. Although the criticism was directed toward LCWR, sisters who were members of congregations belonging to the conference received this very personally. It was heart-breaking to hear some of our most senior sisters raise the question, "What did we do wrong?" This question was usually followed by a list of ministerial experiences they were engaged in on behalf of the church.

> *In some challenging situations one might assume there are bridges to be crossed, but sometimes one might actually need to build the bridge.*

For those who were in Rome to receive the mandate personally, the severity of the document was exacerbated by the knowledge we were separated from our conference members and our communities as the news flooded the airwaves. Although not intended as such, this did turn into a blessing. In the absence of our ordinary ways of communicating with our members, we asked them to grant us a period of prayer, reflection, and a refrain from public comment. This decision came as a surprise to the writers and reporters who were anxious to learn how we would respond. We needed to delve into our contemplative core to discern the way God was inviting us to move forward. To the credit of the many curious writers and reporters, they honored our request.

> *It was a time*
> *When wind and drought destroy, or sweet*
> *spring rains apostatize in sleet,...*
> *a superfluity of dark.*

Yet it was also a time when we internalized invaluable lessons in humility. We learned to be vigilant about conscious and unconsciously held assumptions. We learned to be even more probing in our questioning. In some challenging situations one might assume there are bridges to be crossed, but sometimes one might actually need to build the bridge. We learned that even when unjustly accused, we could trust God to bring us through the night, however long.

Additional Blessings

*O*ther chapters address the unfolding journey of dialogue and discovery, but it is important to speak of the many blessings that became part of the experience.

And yet to take the good
with the warm hands of gratitude.

With such broad media exposure about the experience, it was difficult to anticipate what the public reaction would be. To be sure, some people clearly did not like sisters and especially not sisters who had adopted more contemporary dress and ways of living, following Vatican II. There were also the blogs that reflected unmitigated rancor often attributing the unfortunate actions of one particular sister to every sister who ever lived. While these were very hurtful, they were a very small sample of what really came to us.

The LCWR office and the presidents personally received an overwhelming amount of supportive mail. Thousands upon thousands of letters arrived speaking beautifully of the influence sisters had exerted in their lives. There were letters of deep gratitude and they came with expressions of support, urging us to remain strong amid the controversy.

Too many of the letters spoke of the alienation the writer had experienced with the church as an institution or with some of its ministers. Letter-writers urged us to remain faithful to the LCWR mission and to call the church to integrity and mercy. Sometimes they found their only association with the church to be with the sisters. Our pastoral presence had made a difference in their lives. These letters also deepened our understanding that the way in which we navigated these shoals had implications for many more than ourselves.

Letters came from other organizations. International conferences of religious, both male and female, sent words of support. Letters came from parish priests as well as from persons of other faiths. Initially, it had been difficult to face the daily task of opening the mail. It was not long before bowls with letters from well-wishers grew to overflowing. The LCWR staff prepared binders to hold the letters that came from throughout the world. It was overwhelming. It was humbling. We could only receive this support *with the warm hands of gratitude.*

As beautiful and heart-warming as the letters were, the support did not stop there. The laity came forth with great creativity. Bumper stickers appeared on cars with slogans such as "I support Sisters," or "I love Sisters." Local streets and highways became moving advertisements for their support. This same support was also visible on many of the cars parked in church parking lots on Sunday. This left no doubt in the minds of the clergy as to how many of the laity were reacting to this event.

In 2012 the first LCWR assembly held after the mandate took place in St. Louis. There was a public rally of support for sisters in a park near the arch. There had already been rallies and prayer services in multiple cities throughout the country. There were letters of support on every table at the assembly speaking of the personal encouragement and prayer being offered on our behalf during this time of gathering. There were multiple forms of T-shirts. Groups formed around us to pray with us and for us and many continued to do so on a weekly basis. "Solidarity with Sisters" is one such group that continues to meet today. The laity and sisters from ever so many communities walked closely with us during this time of trial. Members of Solidarity with Sisters organized an event at Catholic University of America to explore the leadership practices utilized by the LCWR presidency and its board. They wanted to learn how such a large organization found ways to hear and incorporate minority opinions. Attendees expressed their desire to learn how the organizations in which they held leadership or membership might become healthier.

> True humility calls for careful and respectful listening. It does not call for cowering or submissiveness.

Although unexpected and unsolicited, many donations came to the LCWR office. A number of those initial donors continue to faithfully give to us. Donors wanted to be sure we had what we needed to secure appropriate legal and canonical advice. Even before the donations began to arrive, we recognized the need for appropriate media training.

The attention of the media was unprecedented for us as an organization. Editorials and articles appeared in *The New York Times, The Washington Post*, and in an abundance of national, international, and local newspapers. Invitations to speak were arriving from multiple organizations, both national and international. LCWR's communications director mediated all requests for interviews or speaking and was an invaluable resource for the necessary preparation of those who would publicly represent LCWR.

When one is trying to work through a crisis in the modality of humility, it is not appropriate to be keeping score as to who is winning and who is losing. We held the attention in our grateful hands. We were also aware that media attention has the potential to work adversely in sensitive situations. That being said, the thoughtful and perceptive material that was put before the public was a gift to us. The media enabled us to speak about our identity and our love for the Gospel and for God's people in ways we could not have accomplished as well on our own. We come once again to the words ....

And yet it is to take the good
with the warm hands of gratitude.

Our hands will ever be warm with gratitude.

The Spiritual Journey and Gift

*S*piritual journeys are special, unique, and perhaps better understood in retrospect than at the time. Even as we worked to engage this challenge with humility, there was both a personal and collective spiritual journey in process. Humility caused us to seek shelter. Humility caused us to seek love. Humility drew us deeper into the heart of God. In so doing, humility became a profound spiritual gift.

It is to have a place to hide
when all is hurricane outside.

Although leaders of religious congregations are often in the public eye, it is generally a more local public and the names of those observing and judging us are often known. This challenge was of an entirely different scope and caliber. The public eye was both national and international. Many, if not most, of those writing or speaking about us were not personally known by us. The challenge of the mandate also invited us, albeit reluctantly, to walk repeatedly through the doors of Vatican offices. These were not pleasure invitations. They were a summons. True humility calls for careful and respectful listening. It does not call for cowering or submissiveness. Holding fast to tension of the two extremes requires vigilance on the part of all invited to the dialogue.

In order to prepare to move forward in this manner, all meetings with those asked to be part of this investigation were preceded by prayer. It was not a quick prayer or even a prayer service. The morning the presidents and executive director went to the appointment with CDF, there were few cues as to what might happen. We sat in silent prayer together for an hour prior to going, asking God's Spirit to be with us and guide us. We had already sent all documentation requested by the bishop charged with the investigation. Prayer and the support of community were our best immediate preparations. We did not realize we were walking right into the eye of the hurricane.

In the weeks and months that followed, the call to individual and communal prayer deepened. How else would one be able to find the wisdom and the strength necessary? Many theologians and canonists came forward to assist us. At times we found ourselves in multiple cities within the same week in order to meet with persons having special expertise. At the same time, our own congregations needed and deserved our leadership and tending. (Although the LCWR executive director worked full-time for the organization, the presidents were serving LCWR in addition to being leaders of their own communities.) Physically, these days were exhausting and stretching. The negative letters and blog posts that did come were often excruciatingly harsh and very public. It was our own scourging at the pillar. It took some time for the very positive support to counteract the negative. Always there were the nagging doubts about the veracity within the negative posts. When one gives one's life in service of God's people, it is for all God's people—not only for those who love us or agree with us.

> There was only one place to go. It was into the arms of God. God was always there. It was God alone who knew of the many tears.

In the midst of all the words, the necessary work, and the feelings, there was a necessity for times of retreat so that each leader could strive to remain grounded. There was only one place to go. It was into the arms of God. God was always there. It was God alone who knew of the many tears. God knew our fears for the conference, for our congregations, and for religious life itself. God knew the toll of the physical and emotional exhaustion. Vatican officials hold considerable power. God heard our many questions and our disappointment in the church to which we had given our lives. God accepted us as we were and provided respite from the public eye. This was the place where we received the grace to pray, not only for ourselves, but for those who were challenging us.

God also sent persons into our lives who were anchors of support. Each of us found ourselves in new and wonderful friendships with wise and deeply caring persons. The cohesiveness of the conference members was a special gift. The allegations that we were less than faithful members of the church had the potential to split the conference. That did not happen.

At the August 2012 LCWR assembly, the first held after the issuance of the mandate, conference members came en masse and filled with emotions. There was considerable rage and outrage. There were those who wondered if there was truth in what they may have read. Conference leadership made the decision there would be room for all voices to be heard. Microphones were placed throughout the room to provide for this input. Long lines formed at the microphones and opinions were often unequivocal. We listened to one another with deep respect. We held the contemplative nature of our dialogue. There was the gradual crafting of a direction for the board and the presidency to follow.

Contemplation has become an integral part of the way in which the conference operates. Contemplation is not an elixir used just to inform us as to the best way to move forward. Contemplation changes the ways in which we do things. It enables us to go deeper. It slows us down. It stills us and better enables us to hear the voice of God.

When one feels wounded, vulnerable, and frightened, love is the balm for those emotions. Once again, love was found in the arms of God. It is not that we had never been there before. The God who laid claim to our hearts had brought us there often. This time there was a greater sense of need and a greater intensity. There was urgency to our presence.

Humility is to have a place
deep in the secret of God's face
where one can know, past all surmise,
that God's great will alone is wise,
where one is loved, where one can trust
a strength not circumscribed by dust.

This is the place where we could come with all our imperfections as well as our gifts. This is the place we feel most at home and most deeply loved. This is the place where trust resides.

Among the many journeys that one can take, some journeys come with great anticipation and joy. Others are journeys through the ordinariness of life. All are important, connected, and become teachers for us. Hard journeys are usually not welcomed. This journey was one we would never have taken, given a choice. Yet there are things that can or may best be learned in the passage of hard journeys that might not be learned elsewhere. This journey taught us skills on many levels. This journey brought us into the company and the support of thousands and thousands of lay persons. Their love and encouragement were gifts to us. This journey brought us to the brink of hopelessness and catastrophe. We learned we could stand on that edge and not fall into the abyss. Whether we represented large congregations or small congregations, we learned to hold the hands of one another. We learned that humility was both a way of navigating and a spiritual gift. We learned that no matter what, we...

"have a place deep in the secret of God's face."

For Reflection and Dialogue

1. Have you ever found yourself in a situation where you thought you had made your position clear, only to discover that other kinds of motivations were being impugned? Can you identify cultural assumptions that might have been present? Are there ways to bridge those different perceptions?

2. Angry response is often an immediate reaction to a perceived injustice or accusation. After reading this chapter, would you ever consider another kind of response? What might that be?

Contemplation stills us and better enables us to hear the voice of God.

10

Making it Through the Long Night, Publicly: Managing Public Information During Crises

Annmarie Sanders, IHM

Christ longs for us to join him, to be one with him,
in communicating across the vast currents of human consciousness
the compassion, the love, the utterly faithful,
total communion that serves as a thickening of grace
that surrounds those who suffer and strengthens them in their inner depths.[1]
-- Constance FitzGerald, OCD

*L*ate in the morning of April 18, 2012, I was boarding a flight in the San Francisco Airport, heading back home to Washington, DC. As I stepped from the jet bridge on to the plane, my cell phone rang with a call from Associated Press national religion writer Rachel Zoll. Since Rachel would only call me if she had a question about LCWR, I wondered what her inquiry could be. After an exchange of pleasantries, the question came: "Does LCWR have any response to the press release?"

"What press release?" I asked, searching back in my mind for any recent story in the news that would relate to LCWR.

A bit taken aback, Rachel responded, "The one released this morning by the USCCB about the CDF doctrinal assessment."

A strong sick feeling surged toward my stomach as I told Rachel that I was not in the office and that this was the first I was hearing of any news on the assessment.

"I am so sorry," Rachel replied. "I didn't realize I would be the person telling you this. The press release is about the doctrinal reform of LCWR that will be undertaken by three US bishops. Do you want me to read the release to you?"

As I stowed my bags and sunk into my seat on the plane, I attempted to take in the enormity of what Rachel was reading to me, growing more incredulous with every sentence. Just as she got to the end, the flight attendant announced it was time to turn off all cell phones. I was left for my cross-country flight with only the words I could retain from the stunning statement I had just tried to absorb: a five-year mandate of reform, three bishops who would oversee LCWR, reviews of all LCWR plans and programs, approval of all speakers at major events. The flight to the east coast seemed endless and over those long hours I grew more confused, angry, and numb.

> How might the way we communicate about this situation add compassion to the currents of human consciousness and contribute to the "thickening of grace"?

As the plane touched down at BWI Airport, I immediately turned on my cell phone and discovered my voicemail could receive no more new messages. As I drove from the airport home, I played the messages in the car – 21 of them – all from reporters seeking a reaction from LCWR to the Vatican's news – CNN, NBC, ABC, BBC, CBS, PBS, major newspapers, national magazines, international news agencies, and an array of radio programs. When I reached home, I began to look at emails: PR agencies, professors, more reporters, and lots of strangers just wanting to reach out to LCWR.

Notably absent was any communication from the LCWR officers in Rome who had directly received the CDF mandate. I was stunned that they had not been in touch. Surely, I thought, they must know we are being bombarded with media inquiries. So why hadn't they called? However, unbeknownst to me, the officers, quietly trying to absorb their experience at CDF and figure out what to do next, had no idea that the document they had just received in a private meeting had by now been studied and scrutinized by media outlets throughout the world, as well as by hundreds, if not thousands of other persons.

April 18, 2012, the day LCWR stepped into a whole new world of international public attention, was a turning point for the conference and for me as its communications director. Our organization had been thrust into the spotlight in a situation that would become a source of interest, consternation, and intrigue to people all over the world. While I was responsible for working with the media on the doctrinal assessment of LCWR since its initiation in 2009, the issuance of the mandate took the story to a whole new level. The challenge of managing public communications for a situation as unanticipated and unprecedented as this loomed large.

Discerning the Call to be Public

As outlined in previous chapters, the extent of discernment that accompanied all decisions about how LCWR would work with the mandate was significant. Often included in this discernment were questions about what to share of this process publicly, as well as when and how to share. Within that discernment, the organization had to ask itself questions such as:

- How do we deal with the allure of public attention?
- How do we not get trapped by the media's desire to make our story their story?
- How can we retain control over how our story is told? Is it possible to control it?
- How might we take advantage of this public interest in women religious and LCWR to speak about this life and the values and vision we hold?
- How might we use this moment to speak publicly for a purpose larger than our own?
- How might the way we communicate about this situation add compassion to the currents of human consciousness and contribute to the "thickening of grace"?

As with most complex situations, drawing easy lines that would define when to share information with others was virtually impossible. In addition, the archbishop delegate and the LCWR leaders agreed not to play out their work on the mandate in the press. Yet there were many times throughout the three years when speaking publicly was essential.

Compounding the situation was the intense attention being given to this situation by people not only throughout the United States, but also throughout the world. As noted in other chapters, the public rallied around Catholic sisters and LCWR by holding protests, prayer vigils, and letter-writing and petition-signing campaigns. Emails, letters, and phone calls streamed into the national office. The messages were often heartfelt sharings not just of gratitude for Catholic sisters and LCWR, but also testimonies of disappointment in positions taken by the Catholic Church. Other conferences of Catholic sisters throughout the world wrote to pledge sisterly support. Non-Catholics who were searching for meaning in their own lives wrote to tell us they could relate to what LCWR was trying to do when raising questions about some of the most important matters facing humanity. Women who had experienced abuse or oppression wrote to express a kinship with LCWR. We were stunned when an LCWR staff member counted the numbers of people who had either sent us letters or emails or signed petitions of support, and found that they totaled nearly 100,000. Clearly, what seemed a private matter between LCWR and CDF had become an issue of serious concern for others far beyond the conference. Besides working with the mandate itself, LCWR realized it needed to face this additional reality – that we also had a responsibility to share at least some of the experience with these thousands of others who were pledging to LCWR their support, often because they identified so closely with our struggle.

The Temptations

As LCWR was thrust into the public light, a number of temptations arose. I list some here since they illuminate the types of questions an organization must continuously discern while going through a similar difficulty.

Temptation #1: Allow the situation to be played out in the media as a story of conflict.

The CDF-LCWR situation had all the makings of a rousing news story. Nothing sells like conflict – especially one that could be portrayed as a battle between a very powerful Vatican office (one formerly known as the Roman Inquisition, no less), who with the backing of the pope, was taking on a group associated for centuries with serving those most in need in society. While there were members of the public who took the side of the Vatican in this matter, vast numbers stood with LCWR. The media, as well as many freelance writers, were all too eager to run with this as another story of women victimized by male church authorities. LCWR, however, was committed to the prevention of further polarization and saw no value for the wider church and world to have this story told in the press in conflictual terms. In addition, we knew that the issues involved in this story were far too complex and vast to be set up as a men-against-women narrative.

Telling a story without demonizing the "other" is a true discipline in today's fast-paced world of short, superficial news. The LCWR officers never underwent a major interview without first practicing how not to fall into traps set by reporters designed to elicit a stinging sound bite that was critical of "the opposition." We saw this in its most dramatic form during a two-and-a-half-hour interview session for the *60 Minutes* segment, "American Nuns Struggle with the Vatican for Change." Although LCWR had agreed to a 45-minute interview of its president, Pat Farrell, OSF, by the late Bob Simon, considered one of the best journalists in the field, the interview went far longer as Mr. Simon tried time after time to draw out critical words from Pat about the church authorities investigating and overseeing LCWR. Pat never took the bait, and her interview during the segment, which aired March 17, 2013, provided solid information about the situation, rather than any attack on another person or side.

Temptation #2: Accept all opportunities to tell the story wherever we can and to whomever will listen.

When LCWR spoke publicly for the first time about the mandate with major news outlets following the meeting of the LCWR board in May 2012, we were amazed by how the stories generated enormous interest in LCWR, an organization virtually unheard of previously by most who were reading, watching, or listening to these stories. The LCWR website was being viewed far more frequently than it had ever been, and a newly created LCWR Facebook page suddenly had hundreds of likes. Most surprisingly, people began to send unsolicited donations to the conference.

> *We were stunned when an LCWR staff member counted the numbers of people who had either written us letters or emails or signed petitions of support, and found that it totaled nearly 100,000.*

Many people wanted to tell the story of the CDF-LCWR experience. As the investigation went on, offers came from freelance writers who saw possibilities of a book. Network and cable news shows wanted to develop features that would delve into the conflict. Invitations even came from satirical news programs such as *The Daily Show* with Jon Stewart and *The Colbert Report*.

Clearly, there were advantages to being out in the news. We began asking ourselves: Should we tell our story as often as we can, especially to audiences who don't know about Catholic sisters? Would this help the mission of religious life today? Would it promote religious life as a vocation choice? If donations continued to pour in, could these unexpected funds be used to promote LCWR's mission in ways that previously were impossible?

As tempting as it was to use every opportunity to speak about religious life and LCWR, our discernment led us to a judicious acceptance of invitations to speak publicly about this situation. We weighed every invitation carefully, always asking what purpose an interview would serve in light of our responsibilities with the CDF mandate. We came to trust that education about religious life and its role in the world would happen in other ways without our needing to keep the CDF story in the media.

Temptation #3: Just let others tell the story.

The conference needed to be the author of its own story. The hard part was that we wanted to tell it according to our own timeline and not that of the media.

From the time of the initiation of the LCWR mandate, the conference made a clear decision – it would not be forced to speak publicly until it was ready, a decision well-documented in previous chapters. Throughout the three years, the presidents would not provide information to the public until they engaged in discernment processes with the conference's board and, whenever possible, engaged in consultative processes with LCWR's approximately 1500 members. These often slow, deliberate processes were frequently a source of frustration to reporters working in the fast-paced news world where being the first to break a story counts mightily.

Often, reporters had an assignment to cover a specific event in the progression of the CDF mandate and, even if LCWR would not speak, wrote a story anyway. They simply found others who had an opinion or an insight into the situation and who were willing to share it publicly.

While many of those who spoke had helpful commentary to offer, none had the full picture of what was happening. So, while tempting to stay out of the fray at times, it became clear that only LCWR could tell its own story. Only LCWR could explain the nuances, the times of silence, the importance of consultation, and how it was attempting to work through this very difficult situation. The conference needed to be the author of its own story. The hard part was that we wanted to tell it according to our own timeline and not that of the media.

Temptation #4: Correct all erroneous statements.

When working with *The New York Times, Washington Post, 60 Minutes,* the *National Catholic Reporter,* and many other well-known, well-staffed media outlets, we had some degree of confidence that facts about our situation would be thoroughly checked and verified before being shared. What was difficult was seeing unsubstantiated allegations against LCWR being made and then repeated by less competent media outlets, as well as by the many columnists, commentators, and bloggers whose words against LCWR were not only highly inaccurate, but hurtful. Although we always had a desire to correct the errors or explain quotes taken far out of context, we decided not to engage in making corrections. The choice to allow erroneous information to stand was hard, but usually seemed wiser than getting into a back and forth with persons who were clearly biased against LCWR and would have most likely used the exchange to perpetuate their negative diatribes about the organization.

Attending to One's Inner Life

*P*revious chapters document that the capacity to deal with these temptations around public communications, as well as all the other challenges that came with the CDF mandate experience, was enhanced through LCWR's efforts to ground all its work in a contemplative stance. This chapter will highlight the importance of those serving as spokespersons or communicators for an organization also to take seriously the responsibility to operate from this deeper source. Viewing one's own situation in relation to a larger whole, attending to movements of the Spirit, identifying how a matter affects the individual, and dealing appropriately with the emotions that arise are key to successfully communicating publicly about a difficult matter with integrity and effectiveness.

Crafting public statements, communicating with our members, prepping the LCWR officers for interviews, dealing with the media, and responding to numerous phone calls, emails, and letters on this matter felt at times for me wrenching, disconcerting, and discouraging. While we strove to keep our communications hope-filled and positive, deep down I often felt beleaguered.

During those three years, I learned that finding appropriate outlets where I could express what I felt as LCWR worked through the mandate – and then finding spaces where I could sort out what I was hearing and experiencing -- was essential. I needed to listen to what was being said by the Vatican and sometimes by the public about LCWR's way of thinking, educating, and communicating and balance that with what I saw within the organization. I knew I needed to do that carefully, responsibly, and humbly to be able to communicate on this difficult matter dispassionately and with integrity.

In addition, as most people working for an organization of which they are not a member probably experience, I often had an opinion and a desire for how I wished a decision would turn out. As a non-member, while I sometimes would be invited to express my opinion during certain deliberations, I had no vote, and no way to impact the eventual outcomes. That reality also needs a contemplative space in which it can be held.

I offer a few practices here that helped me as I attempted to manage LCWR's public communications, especially at times when I sensed some interior conflict or dis-ease about the work I was doing.

1. **Study and learn.** Study connects our personal emotions and personal story to the bigger story of others. While time-consuming, study as much as you can about the topics you are responsible to communicate about. Read with the intention of understanding points of view that differ significantly from your own.

2. **Consider finding consultants** who can advise you as you work. None of us has expertise in all the matters about which we need to communicate. Consider creating a list of people with whom you could speak freely and confidentially about your questions. These may be psychologists, sociologists, scientists, theologians, artists, and more. They may be people whose perspective may not be yours, but whose insights may be important for you to hear and consider. Ask yourself how you need to prepare yourself to be open to their opinions.

3. **Find trusted wisdom figures** in your life with whom you can speak honestly about your own inner self in light of your task. What does it stir in you? Learn how to discern whether you need to set aside your own feelings for the sake of the work you have been asked to do or if the feelings need to be shared.

4. **Give yourself creative, dreaming time.** As hard as this is to do amid the demands placed upon us in our workplaces, these times demand that we find quiet space for thinking broadly, deeply, and freshly. Communications that can make a difference in our society and possibly influence positive change require creativity and imagination to be effective.

5. **Stay as connected as possible with the wider, global world.** Being attentive to the large issues of these times, the struggles of people on every continent, and the questions and hungers people throughout the world carry in their hearts, helps us to look upon our own individual or corporate experiences with greater insight and deeper perspective. Relating our small stories with the much larger narrative of the world helps us see connections and thus participate in building a stronger global community.

April 18, 2012 experiences can come upon any one of us charged with leadership of an organization or its public communications. Since that day in my life, often when I cross over the threshold of a plane, I recall that phone call from Rachel Zoll. Now as I stow my bags and sink into my seat, I stop and think about the difficult and divisive situations that I read about in the day's news or saw on CNN in the airport lounge. I ponder as well how those situations have been reported, and try to reimagine the stories if journalists had crafted them with the intent of creating communion rather than division. As I do, I often recall this part of LCWR's public statement issued after the mandate concluded in 2015:

> *Relating our small stories with the much larger narrative of the world helps us see connections and thus participate in building a stronger global community.*

> From the beginning of LCWR's work with the bishop delegates in 2012, we agreed that we would speak honestly and directly with one another and not through the media. We recognize that this decision frustrated some of our own members, as well as the public and the media. We were highly aware that many people throughout the world were concerned about LCWR and were supporting and praying for us. While at times we too wished we could have shared more along the way with all who cared about this matter, we believe that by keeping our conversations private, we were able to speak with one another at a level of honesty that we believe contributed to the mandate coming to its conclusion as it did. Of utmost importance to us throughout this process was the directive we had received from our own members not to compromise the integrity of LCWR. We believe that integrity was not only kept intact, but perhaps deepened and strengthened through the process.

We acknowledge as well that the doctrinal assessment and mandate deeply disturbed many Catholics and non-Catholics throughout the world. Thousands of people communicated to us their concern, not only for LCWR and Catholic sisters, but for the ramifications these two actions could have for the wider world and church. Many perceived the assessment and mandate as an attempt to suppress the voice of LCWR which was seen as an organization that responsibly raises questions on matters of conscience, faith, and justice. Repeatedly, we heard that people were praying that the manner in which LCWR and the bishop delegates engaged in this process would lead to the creation of safe spaces where matters of such importance could be discussed with openness and honesty, and in an environment freed of fear.

Our hope is that the positive outcome of the assessment and mandate will lead to the creation of additional spaces within the Catholic Church where the church leadership and membership can speak together regularly about the critical matters before all of us. The collective exploration of the meaning and application of key theological, spiritual, social, moral, and ethical concepts must be an ongoing effort for all of us in the world today. Admittedly, entering into a commitment to regular and consistent dialogue about core matters that have the potential to divide us can be arduous, demanding work, but work that is ultimately transformative. However challenging these efforts are, in a world marked by polarities and intolerance of difference, perhaps no work is more important. In an epoch of massive change in the world, we believe such efforts towards ongoing dialogue are fundamental and essential for the sake of our future as a global community. We hope that our years of working through this difficult mandate made some small contribution to this end.

I recall these words as a prayer for all those negotiating global, national, and local situations ridden with division, and for those reporting on them. I recall the words trusting that the efforts undertaken by LCWR's leaders to work through the CDF mandate as they did contributed an energy to the current of consciousness that is now available to others. I imagine leaders, negotiators, journalists, and others worldwide drawing from that current and transforming the ways in which all of us attempt to work through discord and division.

And then, as Constance FitzGerald notes, on the mysterious level of spirit, work done with such intentionality perhaps will "thicken the grace" available for all who suffer in this hurting world.

Endnote

1. Constance FitzGerald, OCD, "Good Friday Reflection," Carmelite Monastery of Baltimore, 2017.

For Reflection and Dialogue

1. Think of a difficult situation connected to your own personal life or work. Would it help you deal with that situation if you see it in relation to a larger whole? Can you identify movements of God's Spirit as you ponder the situation? Does it help you to identify how the matter affects you personally? What might help you to appropriately manage the emotions you experience as you work with that situation?

2. Do any of the practices to attend to one's inner life mentioned here appeal to you as practices you might want to nurture in your life? Are there others that might work well for you?

... on the mysterious level of spirit, work done with such intentionality perhaps will "thicken the grace" available for all who suffer in this hurting world.

11

Discovering Fresh Possibilities in Unexpected Places: Applying What We Witnessed to Our Lives

Betty D. Thompson, Anne M. Regan, and Anna M. Jelen
on behalf of Solidarity with Sisters

Editor's note: *This book would not seem complete without reflection by those not "inside" LCWR, but who were nonetheless impacted by LCWR's experience with the Vatican investigation. To that end, we invited a group of women and men who accompanied LCWR as it worked through the Vatican mandate to write about how that experience has influenced their own lives.*

In April 2012, about 20 people crowded into a living room in Maryland, "furious" or "incredulous" about the new Vatican mandate to reform LCWR. Even those of us who had never been activists were united in determination to publicly oppose the mandate. "We cannot let them get away with this!" said one. Another called it "a perversion of faith, truth, and justice." Many of us linked the mandate to systemic issues in our church: the treatment of women, freedom of conscience, and the hierarchy's detachment from people's experiences and struggles. In contrast, we viewed Catholic sisters as the most effective, credible gospel witnesses in the US church, engaged everywhere in work with people who are vulnerable or marginalized.

All of us are lay Catholic women and men, married and single. No religious sisters or brothers, no priests. But we brought many different energies into the room that first evening. Some arrived alone, knowing no one; others greeted long-time parish acquaintances. Some urged voicing our anger in spirited nonviolent protest. Others steadily advocated a different focus: to express appreciation for and solidarity with Catholic sisters and LCWR, saying, "I felt a debt of gratitude for my education," and "I wanted the sisters to know that the public was behind them and would support them. I wanted them to feel our love in a liberating way."

When we chose to hold a rally rather than a protest, to celebrate Catholic sisters rather than oppose the Vatican's Congregation for the Doctrine of the Faith, we took our first step together toward transformation. We united in a fierce commitment to act strongly, in love. We had no idea what we were getting into, either in the short term or long term. But, as one person said after the rally, "I was ready for action."

The rally day arrived: blue skies, a verdant park beside a busy avenue, and – hooray! – more than 200 people! We prayed, we sang, we heard impressive speakers attest that Catholic sisters embody the Gospel in lives of faithful courage and active love. People found strength, energy, and nourishment in responding to the mandate positively and in community.

Still singing, we marched from the rally to the Vatican Embassy, across from the residence of the Vice President of the United States. Two of us knocked firmly on the embassy's imposing doors. The crowd watched with urgent hope. We wanted the Vatican's ambassador to the US to deliver to Pope Benedict XVI our letter asking for an end to the mandate.

The embassy doors opened! The Vatican's ambassador, Archbishop Carlo Maria Viganó, welcomed two of us inside for a half-hour dialogue. He agreed to convey our letter to the pope. To our amazement, he then invited the organizing team – us! – to join him in quiet prayer in the embassy chapel. Afterwards he came out to the front lawn, with smiles and handshakes for everyone. That experience nudged us away from demonizing or stereotyping people with whom we disagreed.

We knew we wanted to continue this journey in solidarity with LCWR. But how?

We had named ourselves Solidarity with Sisters (SwS) before we even met the women religious at LCWR. From the start, the call to solidarity was the core of what animated us and drew us to action. But we had no outlook wide enough to guess where solidarity with sisters would lead us. We couldn't have imagined the doors that would open and the connections that would beckon us into the heart of the Gospel. Every passage since then has expanded our understanding of solidarity and deepened our commitment to the Holy Spirit in us and among us. We share our story with you to offer an accessible route to hope. We found a way forward that continually asks us to recognize underlying oneness and to discover fresh possibilities in unexpected places. Maybe our experience will help to illuminate your own quest during these challenging times.

Getting Acquainted with LCWR

A few weeks after the rally, the most important door opened to us – the unimposing entry to the LCWR national office. Inside were lasting surprises beyond anything we could have imagined.

Their nonviolence was a commitment to relationship, grounded in spiritual and emotional maturity. We wondered: What did this mean in practice?

We had asked LCWR if we could give them a copy of our rally materials. Warm smiles welcomed us. At the round table in the conference room, as if they had all the time in the world for us, the sisters on the LCWR national office staff listened as we told our story and expressed our support. Then each of them responded personally. They felt our caring and thanked us. We shared hopes and concerns. They invited us to come again. In a mutual relationship of giving and receiving, we still meet with LCWR about every two months, in addition to our own SwS meetings.

When we began, only a few of us counted Catholic sisters as friends, though they had taught many of us, our children, and our parents. Even fewer of us knew anything about LCWR itself. So we eagerly returned to LCWR's simple brick building on a small cul-de-sac. Now the sisters greeted us by name, with glad smiles.

The sisters told us what each of them did to assist LCWR congregations and leaders: publications, leadership training, social justice, annual conferences, business matters. Their voices warmed with esteem and care when they spoke of LCWR's members. We saw the sisters' passion for their ongoing mission even as the mandate claimed far too much of their focus. We were getting acquainted with friendly, wise, merry, strong, vulnerable women. We gradually realized that they were long-time leaders and experts in varied fields. Much easier to see was their consecration of their entire being to life in God. As one of us said, "It is not just about knowing these amazing women, it is what I see them do to actually live gospel values and be church that changes me."

Our diversity added flavor but not hierarchy. The sisters valued the unique persons in the room – teachers, an artist, lawyers, a musician, psychologists, a university professor, senior executives, psychotherapists, an online security expert, a chemist, community organizers, and an editor who was also a professional brewmaster. LCWR and SwS prayed together, shared together, and built relationships of respect, trust, and love.

"Our meetings felt like warmth and light," one of us recalled. The women religious at LCWR's table saw the unique spark in each person in a way that let us see ourselves more fully. This clarity brought fresh grace into our everyday actions. We experienced God alive in each of us. That awareness was like firm and level ground for the journey.

Discovering Another Way of Being

When we arrived at LCWR's door in mid-2012, LCWR was in a time of crisis, discerning how to live with the pain and respond to the challenges of the mandate. We, too, struggled with the Vatican's judgment and oppression. But we struggled differently. Immersed in our confrontational culture, most of us focused on justice for LCWR. How could we urge the Vatican to eliminate the undeserved mandate? In contrast, the sisters focused on genuine mutual understanding and reconciliation. They sought a profoundly nonviolent route to that goal.

Gradually we realized that LCWR defined nonviolence in ways that were radically new to us. Their nonviolence was not a strategy in a campaign of activism. Their nonviolence was a commitment to relationship, grounded in spiritual and emotional maturity. We wondered: What did this mean in practice? Could we absorb lessons that fit our own lives?

LCWR's nonviolence clearly didn't mean weakness. We saw LCWR claim its own integrity, acting with quiet, resourceful restraint. At the same time, the sisters spoke of the bishops always with respectful use of their titles and names, never demeaning or blaming. They were consistently nonconfrontational and nonjudgmental. In our meetings, we saw nonviolence in every aspect of LCWR's communications. For example, when one of us offered a divergent idea, we never heard a skeptical "WHY do you think THAT?!" Instead, the sisters conveyed welcoming curiosity in a simple "Why do you think that?" We recognized the pivotal value of their capacity to ask genuine questions like this and to really hear the answers – not only with us but also in much more challenging situations during the mandate years, as they consulted with LCWR's hundreds of member congregations and met in dialogue with the bishops. As one of us said, "At the LCWR table, we found the capacity to make room for our own truths and those of others – a spaciousness that lets all insights expand." As a reminder that we want to do this, some of us use the term "both/and thinking."

We try to notice if we're excluding or ignoring others; that awareness affects how we listen, whose opinions we seek, and our consciousness of our own privilege.

LCWR's patience and stamina stretched our limits. They accepted ambiguity until something true emerged. In the meantime, they gathered new information without defensiveness or fear. Most of us were used to offering the best answer we had at the moment a question arose. That's efficient, right? It keeps things moving. Slowly we learned to wait until we could name a shared truth or goal. We found the humility to not have an answer. We tried to match LCWR's capacity to love what is broken while imagining wholeness and healing that don't yet exist. We witnessed the sisters' willingness to pay a personal and communal price for that vision.

Through months of conversation during the time of the mandate, we noticed LCWR's persistent, implicit questions. We joined them in asking: What does it mean to live radical love and communal integrity in this situation? What does the Gospel ask of us? In difficult times, we can feel mired in the messes of the world. LCWR's questions offered footholds for forward progress, with Jesus' message of love as our catalyst and guide.

It wasn't easy to make these questions our own. As one of us said, "I had to examine closely my beliefs. It was often difficult to find the words to describe my feelings… to describe my faith. It required a sometimes brutal honesty in trying to discern the truth. Ultimately faith in the guidance of the Spirit was needed because at every step the path ahead was unclear."

In time, we have become more ready to bring open, curious attention to divisions and challenges, without bitterness or hatred. We try to notice if we're excluding or ignoring others; that awareness affects how we listen, whose opinions we seek, and our consciousness of our own privilege. We often take time to sit and pray with an issue, intentionally avoiding a defensive stance or a tendency to react in anger. We can sometimes step back from confrontation and negative judgment. We observe changes in relationships when we "hang tough in a gentle way." We're far from perfect at any of this. But we seriously try – and our meetings keep us focused. We've seen that honest, loving actions and clear, truthful words, combined with a compassionate understanding of the other person's position, can bring about a surprising and good outcome. We're discovering what it means to redeem by love.

We find that the choice of nonviolence is most difficult when we thoughtfully believe that people who have a lot of power are misusing it in ways that harm those who are poor and vulnerable. Can we stay nonjudgmental and nonconfrontational then? Can we find ways to speak truth in love as we work for change? The effort tests our commitment and creativity. Yet in solidarity with LCWR we know that the core of radical nonviolence is a very countercultural belief: that God loves not only us, but also those in conflict with us, equally and extravagantly. We wanted to apply these insights in action.

Finding Our Own Way

*I*n 2012 and 2013, we bit our collective tongue many times as we designed greeting cards to be sent to all active US bishops. The cards would express our views and echo LCWR's way of nonviolence. We wanted to send three sets – for Epiphany, Lent, and Pentecost 2013 – to ask the bishops to advocate for an end to the mandate.

What should we say? We searched for brief words to convey a message that felt almost contradictory. Could we urge the bishops to support LCWR and at the same time express our respect and care for the bishops? What words could hold both truths, in love? We found them, and our artist designed beautiful cards to amplify their themes. Our Epiphany card emphasized the shared prayer in which we and the bishops hold our beloved church and invited them to pray with us "that the doctrinal assessment will be resolved in a way that will inspire the faithful and nourish LCWR leadership." Our Lenten card turned words into a graceful path toward God, and invited the bishops "to join us in the stillness, so that together we might hear God's voice and be open to transformation." In elegant and colorful script, our third card boldly asked the bishops, "filled with the spirit of Pentecost, to stand with us and urge the withdrawal of the 2012 doctrinal assessment." As we folded, signed, stuffed, and stamped more than 1000 cards, it sank in that resolution of the mandate would require more waiting than we had hoped. We received only a few responses. Our support of LCWR would take time.

When we invited the bishops into Lenten stillness, we also chose stillness ourselves. Each Tuesday during Lent 2013, in a small parish chapel, we gathered for prayer to ask God's blessing on LCWR. One of the sisters from LCWR joined us in the chapel. Communal contemplation was new to many of us. Brief opening prayers powerfully led us to an inner silence where we experienced God's presence and solidarity with one another. We felt grounded, deeply peaceful, and connected far beyond ourselves. Brief closing prayers gently wrapped up the experience so we could carry it with us as we left the chapel. During that Lent, Pope Francis was elected. Hope grew wings.

We didn't enter into relationship with LCWR expecting spiritual growth. But it has happened. We have grown in our collective longing for God and our attentiveness to the Holy Spirit. While our personal religious practices still vary, the essence of our spirituality has become more expansive. Some of us had the deep realization that WE are the church as much as those who hold ordained positions and we must be that church to others. Some found a greater call to individual holiness as they confront the core truth of Christ and the Gospel, divine love. The few of us who felt aloof from the church gradually realized that, in solidarity with one another and LCWR, "we're more Catholic than we used to be."

SwS first entered the world in a very public way, at the rally. In the quiet period of cards and chapel contemplation, we found our voice together. Full of flaws and graces, we claimed our individual and communal responsibility to show up in the world as we are. Month by month, we gathered with one another and with LCWR as a community of equals responding to a universal call to holiness. Being in relationship with LCWR and with one another created an implicit accountability; we couldn't ignore the call.

Expanding Our World

*O*ur relationships pulled us into new realizations and bigger realities. For example, we stayed in touch with Archbishop Viganó, the Vatican ambassador. At several times of particularly high international attention to LCWR and of anxiety for us and LCWR, we prayed with him. In the embassy (the first embassy most of us had ever entered), he showed us favorite sculptures. He told us charming stories from his first meeting in Rome with the new Pope Francis. We spoke honestly about serious issues on which we disagreed. Stereotypes of the hierarchy didn't fit this real person. Maybe he, too, got a better sense of real lay people, who knows? How often had a group of progressive lay folks, not vetted by a bishop, come to his door repeatedly to share concerns and hopes?

We recognized relationships through cards and letters, too. In addition to our greeting cards, we wrote letters to two popes, two members of the Roman curia, four bishops and archbishops, and a number of US congregations of women religious. Among the few responses were kind personal replies from women religious, Archbishop Sartain, and a couple of bishops. We came to realize that responses weren't the main point. The big benefit was our change of mind and heart as, again and again, we crafted messages to convey both our strong viewpoints and our genuine care for the recipients. We were making our minds and hearts ready for relationships that cross boundaries – so needed in the world right now.

> We have grown in our collective longing for God and our attentiveness to the Holy Spirit. While our personal religious practices still vary, the essence of our spirituality has become more expansive.

Our website (www.solidaritywithsisters.org), email, Facebook, and Twitter presence aim to be a worldwide offering of relationship. We've tried to write in ways that respect many viewpoints – as if writing to our own cousins with their wide-ranging opinions. Page-views and "Likes" are distant responses to our meditative work of finding and organizing online treasures so others can explore LCWR's ways of leadership, dialogue, action, and reflection. When people visit regularly or comment, distance shrinks and relationships can become mutually supportive.

Our relationship-building took a very personal turn in 2015. After the Orlando LGBTQ massacre, those of us in the same parish asked our pastor if we could hold a "Prayer Vigil for Peace in a Time of Hate and Violence." We were quite uncertain about how he would respond. And then? He took extra steps to publicize the service, he presided himself, and he added warm words of welcome and support throughout the service we had written. He and we became an unexpected team to lead about 75 people in a heartfelt, prayerful time. Two LCWR sisters prayed with us. Movement in a relationship can shift both the present and the future.

Our relationships at LCWR had also changed, becoming true friendships. Our support became personal, like a caring note for the pocket of the executive director during a crucial 2013 meeting, and like our later Mason-jar bouquets for the whole LCWR staff when the mandate was resolved. We pitched in on practical needs, like annually assembling hundreds of member nametags. The artist among us designed a lovely book of photos, artwork, and prayers to appreciate our solidarity with LCWR. And in regular gatherings we absorbed the sisters' certainty that we were already whole and holy, even if some of us didn't feel that way yet.

The mandate had brought us together with LCWR. But our relationship was no longer centered on the mandate. Our presence together in solidarity had become a treasure in itself.

Claiming Our Own Leadership

We were delighted when LCWR decided to publish *Spiritual Leadership for Challenging Times: Presidential Addresses from LCWR* (Orbis, 2014). For quite a while, we had recognized something powerfully special in LCWR's way of leadership – something unique. We asked if we could write discussion questions for public use. Later we also wrote discussion questions for *Transformational Leadership: Conversations with LCWR* (Orbis, 2015). We read the books with care and found connections to our own lives. The books startled us with their candor and wisdom. They told how LCWR has been out in front on many issues since the 1960s. They blazed paths of solidarity with people who are poor, vulnerable, and marginalized. They advocated for the dignity of women everywhere, including women in the church. In LCWR's visions and challenges, we recognized our own.

Both books showed us LCWR's half-century of large-scale organizational leadership during times of constant flux. We recognized their foresight, vision, and courage in making enormous changes as needs evolved. We read of complicated problems in society and in the church that shaped LCWR's creative commitment to systemic solutions. We saw them use that same creativity in responding to the mandate. A big "aha!" was our awareness of how widely LCWR's way of leadership could be applied, far beyond church-based work. Their practices can unlock many "stuck" organizational situations and open unexpected opportunities.

So, around LCWR's table, we proposed that LCWR have a conference to share the wisdom of spiritual leadership. LCWR said no, quite firmly. They suggested we, not they, could lead a conference like that, sharing our own insights. If we wanted, we could invite some women religious to speak, too. So we did.

On the day before Pentecost 2014, 200 people came to Caldwell Hall, a graceful old building at the Catholic University of America. Sunlight poured through the large windows of the conference space, and modern tapestries added color and beauty. Our introductory slides invited everyone to think about leadership. We spoke about our experiences with LCWR. In addresses and on-stage conversations, women religious gave inspiring context and many useful examples of the way of being that we were working to learn. Centering prayer and deep dialogue in small groups invited everyone to consider how these insights could affect their own practices. Music let all voices be heard. Feedback afterwards glowed with the same radiance we felt that day.

> A big "aha!" was our awareness of how widely LCWR's way of leadership could be applied, far beyond church-based work. Their practices can unlock many "stuck" organizational situations and open unexpected opportunities.

Each of us had been growing differently in understanding LCWR's way of leadership. By the end of the conference, we all grasped its essence. LCWR's transformational leadership flows from a unified way of being. Now we could name many intertwined roots of the nonviolence that had puzzled and intrigued us at the beginning of our relationship with LCWR. We connected words like contemplation, discernment, dialogue, meditation, community, work in union with people who are marginalized, welcoming of minority views, prophetic voice, and spiritual or transformational leadership. We felt our genuine solidarity with LCWR.

Each uniquely took LCWR's way of being into our lives. In the process of planning and leading this symposium, we saw our gifts and acted on the responsibilities that go with them, individually and collectively. While we realize that LCWR's mission requires the full effort of the amazing LCWR national office, some of us still imagine how we could work with LCWR to amplify their ways of being and of leadership. Simultaneously, we recognize our own capacity for being and for leading as Solidarity with Sisters.

Recognizing Our Personal and Collective Transformation

All of us smiled in recognition when one recently said, "This way of living calls me to be better than I want to be." The call comes in community. Words from different people express the feelings we share and become a collective quote: "I want to be with these friends as I journey spiritually. We are steadfast companions who challenge, educate, and love together. This journey of solidarity has been deepened by genuine love for each of the women in LCWR and for each member of SwS. It has become a gathering of friends, and a place where wisdom emerges. The process we are going through is truly about personal transformation in order to bring about social transformation."

There's collective transformation, too. Within SwS, being a community rather than a hierarchy is a learning experiment for all of us. There's sometimes tension between decisive, organized approaches and flexible, inclusive approaches. We see many needs that deserve attention; it's seldom obvious which issues to address as SwS. We used to weigh options in traditional ways; now we're likely to wait and listen together with confidence that the right choices will emerge. As time passes, someone regularly reminds us that "contemplation and discernment are well and good, but unless some action is taken, it could be academic." Through the years, we've become more confident in carrying our solidarity into our individual initiatives and letting them, in turn, enrich our solidarity. SwS members have stepped into new work as volunteers, activists, advocates, and discussion leaders.

As a community, we rely on one another. Every time we've jumped into a project, we've found happy surprises as members freely offer talents we didn't know about. New abilities have materialized as needs arose and someone said, "I'll try." Yet even best efforts can leave someone disappointed or vexed. We try to notice and give air to whatever feelings are present, speaking nonconfrontationally, listening nondefensively. Grace and learning have come from tensions when we stay grounded in the vision and love we share. Throughout this chapter, we speak of "a few of us," "many," or "some of us." The underlying story is our movement into wholeness.

In the past few years we've begun a new way of listening to one another. Around LCWR's table, we learned that contemplative dialogue is a very unpretentious process. In a nutshell: We open ourselves to God's presence in us and among us. We read aloud a short insight or reflection and ask ourselves what resonates for me. We sit in silence for at least five minutes. Then we offer brief responses, always with a peaceful pause after each person speaks.

Responses build on one another as we notice connections. We open to the shared meaning unfolding among us – the central dynamic of solidarity.

At first, the pace of contemplative dialogue felt unsettlingly slow. Yet the slower pace creates space for new intimacy and unexpected wisdom. Because of the pauses, we feel called to respond, not react. We open to voices other than our own, including voices we might otherwise dismiss. We appreciate one another more attentively. The pace offers time to absorb what others say, and so each reflection can build on the whole rather than competing with the others. We pay attention to the movement of the Holy Spirit and, together, we create shared space for fresh ideas and innovative solutions. We learn an abiding confidence that, in the group more than individually, truth will emerge. Now our meetings usually include some form of contemplative dialogue, whether with LCWR or SwS alone.

> *T*he pace offers time to absorb what others say, and so each reflection can build on the whole rather than competing with the others…. We learn an abiding confidence that, in the group more than individually, truth will emerge.

In contemplative dialogue, we learn to let the present moment hold our complete attention. We learn to sense the wholeness of all that is – the way God's presence fills both the beauty and the brokenness in our world and in ourselves. This transforms not only us as individuals, but us as a community.

Many of us have found that a contemplative stance seeps into everything. We can be more attentive at home, at work, in prayer, in the search for justice. Sometimes we find we can listen to certain people with equanimity and compassion instead of annoyance. Sometimes we can mentally and emotionally step back from incipient chaos, pause to see it more clearly, and re-enter the situation with a quiet heart and maybe an unexpected thoughtful question.

Contemplative collaboration shaped how we wrote this chapter. Three members volunteered to be the writing team. That team invited everyone to reflect on four questions about our years together so far: why you joined, what you learned, how you changed, why you stay. Twelve members each wrote very personal responses that they shared. The writers constantly held the question of how to be true to these expressions of the Spirit's movements in each of us and among us, often using members' own words. Everyone gave feedback on drafts, twice. At each step, we prayed.

Several members have also incorporated contemplative practices into their work worlds. One finds contemplative options especially useful in making hard decisions that involve a team. He opens space for communal contemplation in simple ways, like inviting quiet pauses in a difficult meeting, or delaying a decision to allow more reflection or to include a wider range of people. He fosters hope that together the group will see an as-yet-unimagined third way, beyond "my way" or "your way." The group's new way forward can address current realities, which may be clearer now than when the project began. Another member proposes that LCWR's communal discernment and collective decision-making are "best practices" that could be translated for wide use in organizations.

We first knocked on LCWR's door to support them in a crisis. Our call has grown way beyond that definition. We walk beside LCWR as it faces challenges and visions very different from the mandate, including reflection on mission and ministries. LCWR sisters walk with us as we face our own challenges and grow in our desire to deepen our spiritual and practical wisdom. Our experience leads us to wonder whether the unique gift women religious of all ages can offer the world right now is their way of being. This is LCWR's great gift to us.

With LCWR and with one another, solidarity has fed our hunger for spiritual life – a hunger that the larger world shares. Many people seem to search for spirituality on their own, without being part of a community questing to live simultaneously in God and in the world. We wish for others to have the remarkable experience of journeying through life in companionship with Catholic sisters or with other people as grounded, mature, and full of grace.

Our companionship with LCWR is transforming, yet our process is simple: regular meetings where we share contemplative time, update one another, and talk about what matters. Our transformation happens as we and these beautiful sisters walk our separate paths together, with ever-growing openness. The sisters at LCWR have very demanding schedules. We juggle many commitments too. Why do we put priority on being together? Is it that we feel the power and beauty of their lives as women religious, and they feel the power and beauty of ours? Is it the unusual and joyous opportunity we create together for intimate conversations between women religious and married and single women and men? Is it our shared, determined hope to be the church of God? Is it our desire to be companions into the unknown future? These questions suggest what solidarity means to all of us, SwS and LCWR. Together we feel the presence of God in a way that strengthens our ability to be agents of love ourselves.

For us, the past five years have been an astonishing privilege and pleasure, an adventure and a learning experience. Our insights unfold even as we write this. What we are able to express will always be incomplete. Some things we know for sure: That it is joyful to be with those who are passionate about their love of God and commitment to serve others. That the Holy Spirit is at work even when we may be unaware of the movement of the Spirit. That the Spirit works in and through groups, not solely through individuals. That contemplation is a powerful gift from God. That God loves not only us, but also those in conflict with us, equally and extravagantly.

However long the night, we were made for these times.

*The reflections that formed the foundation of this chapter were written by **Susan De Quattro, Linda Plitt Donaldson, Bill Fanelli, Anna M. Jelen, Arlene McGarrity, Richard McGinnis, Mary D. Ott, Anne M. Regan, Judith Sholes, Joan Marie Sklamm, Stuart Sklamm,** and **Betty D. Thompson**.*

For Reflection and Dialogue

1. As this group of women and men who accompanied LCWR during a time of crisis named how that experience is impacting their lives, how would you say your life has been impacted by the material in this book?

2. Is there any new practice, different way of being, or changed perspective that you wish to incorporate into your own life? How might you begin that incorporation?

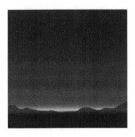

Epilogue

Joan Marie Steadman, CSC

As we reflect on the journey we made, not by ourselves, but with all with whom we were in relationship through the doctrinal assessment of LCWR, the issuing of the mandate, and its resolution the words that well up within us are: "Nothing can separate us from the love of Christ," "My love and my grace are enough for you," and "God can do infinitely more than we can ask or imagine." These words hold a promise that sustained us in our personal and communal journeys. They were made real at each step along the way as a journey that began in darkness unfolded into light. We walked together along a path that was revealed one step at a time and the strength, wisdom, compassion, and openness needed were given in each of those moments.

There is a longing in the hearts of many for spaces and places where contemplation, dialogue, and discernment bring us together. We long to be able to build bridges across the chasms that can divide us. Pope Francis challenges us to be a church and a people for whom contemplation, dialogue, and discernment are a way of life -- a way of life that enables us to create a culture of encounter in which we are open to the ever-present Spirit of God transforming human hearts and relationships and the graced unfolding of all creation.

Prayer, support, and friendship sustained us on the journey we have shared with you. As we look back we see the threads of grace and light that can only be discerned with some distance from the immediate experience. We responded as we did out of love and for the sake of the church and the global community. We hope that what we have shared in this book will support you in your response to the call to build a world where mercy, love, justice, peace, and forgiveness bind us together.

The Authors

Creating this book was an experience of dialogue and communal discernment over the course of more than two years.
Part of the experience was a writing retreat that took place at the Oblate Renewal Center in San Antonio, Texas where the authors spent several days in prayer and reflection as we wrote and gave feedback to one another on our chapters. While each chapter is written by one or two of us, in reality, each one is a creaton of all of us.

Here on the renewal center grounds are: (left to right): Marlene Weisenbeck, FSPA; Janet Mock, CSJ; Pat Farrell, OSF; Sharon Holland, IHM; Florence Deacon, OSF; Marcia Allen, CSJ; Carol Zinn, SSJ; Mary Hughes, OP; Joan Marie Steadman, CSC; and Annmarie Sanders, IHM.

Marcia Allen, CSJ

Marcia is a member of the Sisters of St. Joseph of Concordia, Kansas. She holds bachelor of arts degrees in history and French, a master of science in administration and a doctorate of ministry in spirituality. She served four terms as president of her community and was in the presidency of LCWR from 2014 -2017. She is a practiced facilitator and process designer for congregational meetings. At present she serves as retreat director and spiritual companion at the Manna House of Prayer.

Florence Deacon, OSF

Florence is a member of the Sisters of St. Francis of Assisi in St. Francis, Wisconsin. She has a doctorate from the women's history program at the University of Wisconsin with a minor in African history, and has ministered as a middle school teacher, a history and political science professor at Cardinal Stritch University, and director of the New York Office of Franciscans International, representing Franciscans from around the world at the United Nations. She was ministering as the justice coordinator for the Society of the Holy Child Jesus in Pennsylvania when she was elected to lead her congregation. She served in the LCWR presidency from 2011-2014 and is currently the congregation justice coordinator for the Sisters of the Holy Cross in Notre Dame, Indiana.

Pat Farrell, OSF

Pat is a Franciscan from Dubuque, Iowa. She has served in a variety of ministries, including religious education, community organizing, secondary education, and mental health work. She is a long-time missioner who served for 20 years in Chile and El Salvador. As a licensed clinical social worker, her therapy has focused primarily on trauma recovery with survivors of war and torture as well as work with religious. In 2008 Pat was elected to leadership in her congregation and served in the LCWR presidency from 2010-2013. She is currently living and working in Honduras doing counseling, spiritual direction, and prison ministry.

Sharon Holland, IHM

Sharon is a member of the Sisters, Servants of the Immaculate Heart of Mary of Monroe, Michigan. She holds an undergraduate degree in music from Marygrove College, a graduate degree in religious studies from the University of Detroit, and a doctorate (JCD) in canon law from the Gregorian University in Rome. From 1988-2009 she served on the staff, and as an office head at the Vatican Office for Consecrated Life (CICLSAL). While in Rome, she also taught canon law to international groups of sisters at the Pontifical Institute, Regina Mundi, and was a consultant to religious congregations and to sponsored ministries in health care and higher education. She was elected to her congregation's leadership team in 2012, and served from 2013-2016 in the presidency of LCWR.

Mary Hughes, OP

Mary, a Dominican Sister of Amityville, currently serves as the LCWR director of transitional services. She holds an undergraduate degree in English and elementary education, a graduate degree in early childhood education, and a graduate degree and a doctor of education in curriculum and teaching. Much of her ministerial background has been in the field of education, and twice she served as the prioress of her community. She served in the LCWR presidency from 2009-2012. She also serves now as an adjunct professor at Fordham University, teaching a course on the spirituality of leadership.

Anna M. Jelen

Anna was educated by the Dominican Sisters for 12 years and the Sisters of the Holy Cross for two years. These women religious were a positive but unacknowledged presence in her early life. When she joined Solidarity with Sisters, she found that she could acknowledge the work of sisters and support them in their efforts to resolve the CDF mandate. She has been a wife, mother, grandmother, teacher of high school English, and an assistant editor.

Janet Mock, CSJ

Janet is a Sister of St. Joseph of Baden, Pennsylvania. She has been an educator, a formation director, and was in congregational leadership in her religious community. Following congregational leadership, she worked in community outreach at Carlow Hill College in the Hill District of Pittsburgh for five years. She later served as executive director of the Religious Formation Conference, director of leadership and mission at Washington Theological Union, and executive director of LCWR from 2011-2014. She is currently campus outreach coordinator at the motherhouse of the Sisters of St. Joseph in Baden.

Anne Regan

Anne is a psychologist in private practice in Silver Spring, Maryland. Her participation with Solidarity with Sisters has illuminated how deeply her life has been informed by generations of women religious. Her work with individuals, couples, and organizations is committed to the restoration of wholeness in the service of human liberation.

Annmarie Sanders, IHM

Annmarie has been serving as the LCWR director of communications since 2003. She had previously worked in communications for her congregation (Sisters, Servants of the Immaculate Heart of Mary in Scranton, Pennsylvania), Marywood College, and in Peru for *Latinamerica Press/Noticias Aliadas*. Prior to this she was a medical social worker. She holds an undergraduate degree in social work and a graduate degree in public communications. She edited *Spiritual Leadership for Challenging Times: Presidential Addresses of the Leadership Conference of Women Religious* (Orbis Books, 2014) and *Transformational Leadership: Conversations with the Leadership Conference of Women Religious* (Orbis Books, 2015).

Joan Marie Steadman, CSC

Joan Marie is a Sister of the Holy Cross of Notre Dame, Indiana. She served as the LCWR executive director from 2015-2017, after completing 15 years of leadership for her congregation. Some of her previous ministries have included: associate director of healthcare ethics at the Markula Center for Applied Ethics at Santa Clara University; vice-president for mission at Holy Cross Hospital, Salt Lake City, Utah; regional executive team member at Holy Cross Health Services of Utah; and service as a pastoral associate, school administrator and teacher, and novice director for her community. She holds a bachelor of science degree in biology and a master of arts degree in spirituality.

Betty D. Thompson

Betty is a wife, mother, and grandmother, educated by women religious from first grade through high school before receiving a bachelor of arts in history, with studies at Fordham and Marquette Universities. For 34 years, Betty worked to nudge the US Department of Housing and Urban Development toward better processes, communications, and customer focus. She manages the website, Facebook, Twitter, and email for Solidarity with Sisters. She also works to advance accessibility for people with disabilities.

Marlene Weisenbeck FSPA

Marlene is a Franciscan Sister of Perpetual Adoration from La Crosse, Wisconsin with undergraduate and graduate degrees in music, a licentiate in canon law, and a doctorate in higher education administration. Besides serving in the presidency of LCWR from 2008-2011, she has also served in numerous other leadership roles, namely president of her congregation (2002-2010), president of the National Conference of Vicars for Religious (1998-2000), and chair of the Viterbo University Board (1994-2002). She is the founder of the La Crosse Task Force to End Modern Slavery (2013) and is currently working to raise awareness about human trafficking, assisting victims, and serving with other organizations sharing the same goals.

Carol Zinn, SSJ

Carol is a Sister of Saint Joseph from Philadelphia, Pennsylvania and has served in the ministry of education, at the UN-NGO representing Sisters of Saint Joseph around the world, in congregational leadership, and in the LCWR presidency from 2012-2015. She currently serves as senior vice-president for mission integration at Plante Moran CRESA working with leadership teams and members on preferred future planning. She holds an undergraduate degree in education, a graduate degree in theology, and a doctorate in curriculum development and foundations of American education.

Glossary

Apostolic nuncio – some nations which have diplomatic relations with the Holy See have adopted a protocol under which the Vatican ambassador automatically holds the rank of dean of the diplomatic corps in their country. In those nations, such as the United States, the papal envoy is called an apostolic nuncio.

Code of Canon Law: the system of laws and legal principles governing the Catholic Church

Curia: the church's central administrative offices

Dicastery: a department of the Curia

Holy See: refers to the pope and the administrative offices in their role of authority over and service to the Catholic Church around the world

Magisterium: can refer to the authority that the pope and the bishops have to teach, or can refer to the content of what is authoritatively taught

Prefect: the title given to cardinals who head Vatican congregations

Public juridic persons: artificial entities (aggregates or groupings of persons or things) created by the church that are conferred with certain rights and have certain obligations to carry out the mission of the church that is entrusted to them.

Religious order or religious congregation: an institute of men or women who take vows of poverty, chastity, and obedience, living under a common rule.

Woman religious: another term for Catholic sister. A sister is a woman who professes perpetual vows, most commonly of poverty, chastity, and obedience. Because a sister belongs to a form of life called religious life, she can also be called a "woman religious." (Women religious use the formal title Sister, with the initials of the religious community to which they belong following their name, i.e., Sister Mary Smith, OSF. In this book, we do not use the title Sister, but rather just the name and initials – Mary Smith, OSF.)

Appendices

Appendix A

The following is the text of what is referred to in this book as "the mandate." It is the document presented on April 18, 2012 to the officers of the Leadership Conference of Women Religious as they met at the Vatican with representatives of the Congregation for the Doctrine of the Faith. This document was posted to the public side of the website of the US Catholic Conference of Bishops moments after the meeting of the CDF and LCWR officials ended.

Congregatio Pro Doctrina Fidei

Doctrinal Assessment of the Leadership Conference of Women Religious

I. Introduction

The context in which the current doctrinal Assessment of the Leadership Conference of Women Religious in the United States of America is best situated is articulated by Pope John Paul II in the Post-Synodal Apostolic Exhortation *Vita consecrata* of 1996. Commenting on the genius of the charism of religious life in the Church, Pope John Paul says: *"In founders and foundresses we see a constant and lively sense of the Church, which they manifest by their full participation in all aspects of the Church's life, and in their ready obedience to the Bishops and especially to the Roman Pontiff. Against this background of love towards Holy Church 'the pillar and bulwark of truth' (1 Tim 3:15), we readily understand... the full ecclesial communion which the Saints, founders and foundresses, have shared in diverse and often difficult times and circumstances. They are examples which consecrated persons need constantly to recall if they are to resist the particularly strong centrifugal and disruptive forces at work today. A distinctive aspect of ecclesial communion is allegiance of mind and heart to the Magisterium of the Bishops, an allegiance which must be lived honestly and clearly testified to before the People of God by all consecrated persons, especially those involved in theological research, teaching, publishing, catechesis and the use of the means of social communication. Because consecrated persons have a special place in the Church, their attitude in this regard is of immense importance for the whole People of God"* (n. 46).

The Holy See acknowledges with gratitude the great contribution of women Religious to the Church in the United States as seen particularly in the many schools, hospitals, and institutions of support for the poor which have been founded and staffed by Religious over the years. Pope John Paul II expressed this gratitude well in his meeting with Religious from the United States in San Francisco on September 17, 1987, when he said: *I rejoice because of your deep love of the Church and your generous service to God's people...The extensive Catholic educational and health care systems, the highly developed network of social services in the Church - none of this would exist today, were it not for your highly motivated dedication and the dedication of those who have gone before you. The spiritual vigor of so many Catholic people testifies to the efforts of generations of religious in this land. The history of the Church in this country is in large measure your history at the service of God's people.* The renewal of the Leadership Conference of Women Religious which is the goal of this doctrinal Assessment is in support of this essential charism of Religious which has been so obvious in the life and growth of the Catholic Church in the United States.

While recognizing that this doctrinal Assessment concerns a particular conference of major superiors and therefore does not intend to offer judgment on the faith and life of Women Religious in the member Congregations which belong to that conference, nevertheless the Assessment reveals serious doctrinal problems which affect many in Consecrated Life. On the doctrinal level, this crisis is characterized by a diminution of the fundamental Christological center and focus of religious consecration which leads, in turn, to a loss of a "constant and lively sense of the Church" among some Religious. The current doctrinal Assessment arises out of a sincere concern for the life of faith in some Institutes of Consecrated Life and Societies of Apostolic Life. It arises as well from a conviction that the work of any conference of major superiors of women Religious can and should be a fruitful means of addressing the contemporary situation and supporting religious life in its most "radical" sense—that is, in the faith in which it is rooted. According to Canon Law, conferences of major superiors are an expression of the collaboration between the Holy See, Superiors General, and the local Conferences of Bishops in support of consecrated life. The overarching concern of the doctrinal Assessment is, therefore, to assist the Leadership Conference of Women Religious in the United States in implementing an ecclesiology of communion founded on faith in Jesus Christ and the Church as the essential foundation for its important service to religious Communities and to all those in consecrated life.

II. The doctrinal Assessment

The decision of the Congregation for the Doctrine of the Faith (CDF) to undertake a doctrinal Assessment of the Leadership Conference of Women Religious (LCWR) was communicated to the LCWR Presidency during their meeting with Cardinal William Levada in Rome on April 8, 2008. At that meeting, three major areas of concern were given as motivating the CDF's decision to initiate the Assessment:

- **Addresses at the LCWR Assemblies.** Addresses given during LCWR annual Assemblies manifest problematic statements and serious theological, even doctrinal errors. The Cardinal offered as an example specific passages of Sr. Laurie Brink's address about some Religious "moving beyond the Church" or even beyond Jesus. This is a challenge not only to core Catholic beliefs; such a rejection of faith is also a serious source of scandal and is incompatible with religious life. Such unacceptable positions routinely go unchallenged by the LCWR, which should provide resources for member Congregations to foster an ecclesial vision of religious life, thus helping to correct an erroneous vision of the Catholic faith as an important exercise of charity. Some might see in Sr. Brink's analysis a phenomenological snapshot of religious life today. But Pastors of the Church should also see in it a cry for help.

- **Policies of Corporate Dissent.** The Cardinal spoke of this issue in reference to letters the CDF received from "Leadership Teams" of various Congregations, among them LCWR Officers, protesting the Holy See's actions regarding the question of women's ordination and of a correct pastoral approach to ministry to homosexual persons, e.g. letters about New Ways Ministry's conferences. The terms of the letters suggest that these sisters collectively take a position not in agreement with the Church's teaching on human sexuality. It is a serious matter when these Leadership Teams are not providing effective leadership and example to their communities, but place themselves outside the Church's teaching.

- **Radical Feminism.** The Cardinal noted a prevalence of certain radical feminist themes incompatible with the Catholic faith in some of the programs and presentations sponsored by the LCWR, including theological interpretations that risk distorting faith in Jesus and his loving Father who sent his Son for the salvation of the world. Moreover, some commentaries on "patriarchy" distort the way in which Jesus has structured sacramental life in the Church; others even undermine the revealed doctrines of the Holy Trinity, the divinity of Christ, and the inspiration of Sacred Scripture.

Subsequently, in a letter dated February 18, 2009, the CDF confirmed its decision to undertake a doctrinal Assessment of the LCWR and named Most Rev. Leonard Blair, Bishop of Toledo, as the CDF's Delegate for the Assessment.

This decision was further discussed with the LCWR Presidency during their visit to the CDF on April 22, 2009. During that meeting, Cardinal Levada confirmed that the doctrinal Assessment comes as a result of several years of examination of the doctrinal content of statements from the LCWR and of their annual conferences. The Assessment's primary concern is the doctrine of the faith that has been revealed by God in Jesus Christ, presented in written form in the divinely inspired Scriptures, and handed on in the Apostolic Tradition under the guidance of the Church's Magisterium. It is this Apostolic teaching, so richly and fully taught by the Second Vatican Council, that should underlie the work of a conference of major superiors of Religious which, by its nature, has a canonical relationship to the Holy See and many of whose members are of Pontifical right.

Most Rev. Leonard Blair communicated a set of doctrinal *Observations* to the LCWR in a letter dated May 11, 2009, and subsequently met with the Presidency on May 27, 2009. The LCWR Presidency responded to the *Observations* in a letter dated October 20, 2009. Based on this response, and on subsequent correspondence between the Presidency of the LCWR and the Delegate, Bishop Blair submitted his findings to the CDF on December 22, 2009.

On June 25, 2010, Bishop Blair presented further documentation on the content of the LCWR's *Mentoring Leadership Manual* and also on the organizations associated with the LCWR, namely *Network* and *The Resource Center for Religious Institutes.* The documentation reveals that, while there has been a great deal of work on the part of LCWR promoting issues of social justice in harmony with the Church's social doctrine, it is silent on the right to life from conception to natural death, a question that is part of the lively public debate about abortion and euthanasia in the United States. Further, issues of crucial importance to the life of Church and society, such as the Church's Biblical view of family life and human sexuality, are not part of the LCWR agenda in a way that promotes Church teaching. Moreover, occasional public statements by the LCWR that disagree with or challenge positions taken by the Bishops, who are the Church's authentic teachers of faith and morals, are not compatible with its purpose.

All of the documentation from the doctrinal Assessment including the LCWR responses was presented to the Ordinary Session of the Cardinal and Bishop Members of the CDF on January 12, 2011. The decision of that Ordinary Session was:

1) The current doctrinal and pastoral situation of the LCWR is grave and a matter of serious concern, also given the influence the LCWR exercises on religious Congregations in other parts of the world;

2) After the currently-ongoing Visitation of religious communities of women in the United States is brought to a conclusion, the Holy See should intervene with the prudent steps necessary to effect a reform of the LCWR;

3) The Congregation for the Doctrine of the Faith will examine the various forms of canonical intervention available for the resolution of the problematic aspects present in the LCWR.

The Holy Father, Pope Benedict XVI, in an Audience granted to the Prefect of the Congregation for the Doctrine of the Faith, Cardinal William Joseph Levada, on January 14, 2011, approved the decisions of the Ordinary Session of the Congregation, and ordered their implementation. This action by the Holy Father should be understood in virtue of the mandate given by the Lord to Simon Peter as the rock on which He founded his Church (cf. Luke 22:32): "I have prayed for you, Peter, that your faith may not fail; and when you have turned to me, you must strengthen the faith of your brothers and sisters." This Scripture passage has long been applied to the role of the Successors of Peter as Head of the Apostolic College of Bishops; it also applies to the role of the Pope as Chief Shepherd and Pastor of the Universal Church. Not least among the flock to whom the Pope's pastoral concern is directed are women Religious of apostolic life, who through the past several centuries have been so instrumental in building up the faith and life of the Holy Church of God, and witnessing to God's love for humanity in so many charitable and apostolic works.

Since the Final Report of the Apostolic Visitation of women Religious in the United States has now been submitted to the Holy See (in December, 2011), the CDF turns to the implementation of the above-mentioned decisions approved by the Holy Father as an extension of his pastoral outreach to the Church in the United States. For the purpose of this implementation, and in consultation with the Congregation for Institutes of Consecrated Life and Societies of Apostolic Life (CICLSAL) and the Congregation for Bishops, the Congregation for the Doctrine of the Faith has decided to execute the mandate to assist in the necessary reform of the Leadership Conference of Women Religious through the appointment of a Archbishop Delegate, who will – with the assistance of a group of advisors (bishops, priests, and women Religious) – proceed to work with the leadership of the LCWR to achieve the goals necessary to address the problems outlined in this statement. The mandate given to the Delegate provides the structure and flexibility for the delicate work of such implementation.

The moment for such a common effort seems all the more opportune in view of an implementation of the recommendations of the recent Apostolic Visitation of women Religious in the United States, and in view of this year's 50th anniversary of the beginning of the Second Vatican Council, whose theological vision and practical recommendations for Consecrated Life can serve as a providential template for review and renewal of religious life in the United States, and of the mandate of Church law for the work of this conference of major superiors to which the large majority of congregations of women Religious in the United States belong.

III. Implementation: Conclusions of Doctrinal Assessment and Mandate

1) Principal Findings of the Doctrinal Assessment

LCWR General Assemblies, Addresses, and Occasional Papers

One of the principal means by which the LCWR promotes its particular vision of religious life is through the annual Assemblies it sponsors. During the Assessment process, Bishop Blair, in his letter of May 11, 2009, presented the LCWR Presidency with a study and doctrinal evaluation of keynote addresses, presidential addresses, and Leadership Award addresses over a 10 year period. This study found that the talks, while not scholarly theological discourses *per se*, do have significant doctrinal and moral content and implications which often contradict or ignore magisterial teaching.

In its response, the Presidency of the LCWR maintained that it does not knowingly invite speakers who take a stand against a teaching of the Church "when it has been declared as authoritative teaching." Further, the Presidency maintains that the assertions made by speakers are their own and do not imply intent on the part of the LCWR. Given the facts examined, however, this response is inadequate. The Second Vatican Council clearly indicates that an authentic teaching of the Church calls for the religious submission of intellect and will, and is not limited to defined dogmas or *ex cathedra* statements (cf. *Lumen gentium*, 25). For example, the LCWR publicly expressed in 1977 its refusal to assent to the teaching of *Inter insigniores* on the reservation of priestly ordination to men. This public refusal has never been corrected. Beyond this, the CDF understands that speakers at conferences or general assemblies do not submit their texts for prior review by the LCWR Presidency. But, as the

Assessment demonstrated, the sum of those talks over the years is a matter of serious concern.

Several of the addresses at LCWR conferences present a vision or description of religious life that does not conform to the faith and practice of the Church. Since the LCWR leadership has offered no clarification about such statements, some might infer that such positions are endorsed by them. As an entity approved by the Holy See for the coordination and support of religious Communities in the United States, LCWR also has a positive responsibility for the promotion of the faith and for providing its member Communities and the wider Catholic public with clear and persuasive positions in support of the Church's vision of religious life.

Some speakers claim that dissent from the doctrine of the Church is justified as an exercise of the prophetic office. But this is based upon a mistaken understanding of the dynamic of prophecy in the Church: it justifies dissent by positing the possibility of divergence between the Church's magisterium and a "legitimate" theological intuition of some of the faithful. "Prophecy," as a methodological principle, is here directed *at* the Magisterium and the Church's pastors, whereas true prophecy is a grace which accompanies the exercise of the responsibilities of the Christian life and ministries within the Church, regulated and verified by the Church's faith and teaching office. Some of the addresses at LCWR-sponsored events perpetuate a distorted ecclesiological vision, and have scant regard for the role of the Magisterium as the guarantor of the authentic interpretation of the Church's faith.

The analysis of the General Assemblies, Presidential Addresses, and *Occasional Papers* reveals, therefore, a two-fold problem. The first consists in positive error (i.e. doctrinally problematic statements or formal refutation of Church teaching found in talks given at LCWR-sponsored conferences or General Assemblies). The second level of the problem concerns the silence and inaction of the LCWR in the face of such error, given its responsibility to support a vision of religious life in harmony with that of the Church and to promote a solid doctrinal basis for religious life. With this Assessment, the CDF intends to assist the LCWR in placing its activity into a wider context of religious life in the universal Church in order to foster a vision of consecrated life consistent with the Church's teaching. In this wider context, the CDF notes the absence of initiatives by the LCWR aimed at promoting the reception of the Church's teaching, especially on difficult issues such as Pope John Paul II's Apostolic Letter *Ordinatio sacerdotalis* and Church teaching about homosexuality.

The Role of the LCWR in the Doctrinal Formation of Religious Superiors and Formators

The program for new Superiors and Formators of member Communities and other resources provided to these Communities is an area in which the LCWR exercises an influence. The doctrinal Assessment found that many of the materials prepared by the LCWR for these purposes (*Occasional Papers, Systems Thinking Handbook*) do not have a sufficient doctrinal foundation. These materials recommend strategies for dialogue, for example when sisters disagree about basic matters of Catholic faith or moral practice, but it is not clear whether this dialogue is directed towards reception of Church teaching. As a case in point, the *Systems Thinking Handbook* presents a situation in which sisters differ over whether the Eucharist should be at the center of a special community celebration since the celebration of Mass requires an ordained priest, something which some sisters find "objectionable." According to the *Systems Thinking Handbook* this difficulty is rooted in differences at the level of belief, but also in different cognitive models (the "Western mind" as opposed to an "Organic mental model"). These models, rather than the teaching of the Church, are offered as tools for the resolution of the controversy of whether or not to celebrate Mass. Thus the *Systems Thinking Handbook* presents a neutral model of Congregational leadership that does not give due attention to the responsibility which Superiors are called to exercise, namely, leading sisters into a greater appreciation or integration of the truth of the Catholic faith.

The Final Report of the Apostolic Visitation of Religious Communities of Women in the United States (July, 2011) found that the formation programs among several communities that belong to the LCWR did not have significant doctrinal content but rather were oriented toward professional formation regarding particular issues of ministerial concern to the Institute. Other programs reportedly stressed their own charism and history, and/or the Church's social teaching or social justice in general, with little attention to basic Catholic doctrine, such as that contained in the authoritative text of the *Catechism of the Catholic Church*. While these formation programs were not directly the object of this doctrinal Assessment, it may nevertheless be concluded that confusion about the Church's authentic doctrine of the faith is reinforced, rather than corrected, by the lack of doctrinal content in the resources provided by the LCWR for Superiors and Formators. The doctrinal confusion which has undermined solid catechesis over the years demonstrates the need for sound doctrinal formation—both initial and ongoing—for women Religious and novices just as it does for priests and seminarians, and for laity in ministry and apostolic life. In this way, we can hope that the secularized contemporary culture, with its negative impact on the very identity of Religious as Christians and members of the Church, on their religious practice and common life, and on their authentic Christian spirituality, moral life, and liturgical practice, can be more readily overcome.

2) The Mandate for Implementation of the Doctrinal Assessment

In the universal law of the Church (Code of Canon Law [C.I.C.] for the Latin Church), Canons 708 and 709 address the establishment and work of conferences of major superiors:

Can. 708: Major superiors can be associated usefully in conferences or councils so that by common efforts they work to achieve more fully the purpose of the individual institutes, always without prejudice to their autonomy, character, and proper spirit, or to transact common affairs, or to establish appropriate coordination and cooperation with the conferences of bishops and also with individual bishops.

Can. 709: Conferences of major superiors are to have their own statutes approved by the Holy See, by which alone they can be erected even as a juridic person and under whose supreme direction they remain.

In the light of these canons, and in view of the findings of the doctrinal Assessment, it is clear that greater emphasis needs to be placed both on the relationship of the LCWR with the Conference of Bishops, and on the need to provide a sound doctrinal foundation in the faith of the Church as they "work to achieve more fully the purpose of the individual institutes."

Therefore in order to implement a process of review and conformity to the teachings and discipline of the Church, the Holy See, through the Congregation for the Doctrine of the Faith, will appoint an Archbishop Delegate, assisted by two Bishops, for review, guidance and approval, where necessary, of the work of the LCWR. The Delegate will report to the CDF, which will inform and consult with the Congregation for Institutes of Consecrated Life and Societies of Apostolic Life and the Congregation for Bishops.

The mandate of the Delegate is to include the following:

1) To revise LCWR Statutes to ensure greater clarity about the scope of the mission and responsibilities of this conference of major superiors. The revised Statutes will be submitted to the Holy See for approval by the CICLSAL.

2) To review LCWR plans and programs, including General Assemblies and publications, to ensure that the scope of the LCWR's mission is fulfilled in

accord with Church teachings and discipline. In particular:

- *Systems Thinking Handbook* will be withdrawn from circulation pending revision

- LCWR programs for (future) Superiors and Formators will be reformed

- Speakers/presenters at major programs will be subject to approval by Delegate

3) To create new LCWR programs for member Congregations for the development of initial and ongoing formation material that provides a deepened understanding of the Church's doctrine of the faith.

4) To review and offer guidance in the application of liturgical norms and texts. For example:

-The Eucharist and the Liturgy of the Hours will have a place of priority in LCWR events and programs.

5) To review LCWR links with affiliated organizations, e.g. Network and Resource Center for Religious Life.

The mandate of the Delegate will be for a period of up to five years, as deemed necessary. In order to ensure the necessary liaison with the USCCB (in view of Can. 708), the Conference of Bishops will be asked to establish a formal link (e.g. a committee structure) with the Delegate and Assistant Delegate Bishops. In order to facilitate the achievement of these goals, the Delegate is authorized to form an Advisory Team (clergy, women Religious, and experts) to assist in the work of implementation.

It will be the task of the Archbishop Delegate to work collaboratively with the officers of the LCWR to achieve the goals outlined in this document, and to report on the progress of this work to the Holy See. Such reports will be reviewed with the Delegate at regular interdicasterial meetings of the CDF and the CICLSAL. In this way, the Holy See hopes to offer an important contribution to the future of religious life in the Church in the United States.

Appendix B

Public Statement of the Leadership Conference of Women Religious Regarding CDF Report

August 10, 2012

[**St. Louis, MO**]   At the annual assembly of the Leadership Conference of Women Religious (LCWR) held in St. Louis, MO, August 7-10, the 900 participants planned their response to the doctrinal assessment of the organization by the Congregation for the Doctrine of the Faith (CDF).

As the meeting took place, participants were reminded of the thousands of people throughout the country and the world who had been communicating with LCWR since the CDF report was issued on April 18, urging that the response be one that helps to reconcile the differences that exist within the Catholic Church and creates spaces for honest and open conversation on the critical moral and ethical questions that face the global community. Since receiving the CDF report, the LCWR officers made efforts to hear the voices of as many of its 1500 members as possible by inviting them into processes of prayerful consideration of the report's findings and recommendations. Members then gathered in regional meetings throughout the country to share their insights, which became the basis for the conversations that took place at this assembly, which was the first gathering of the majority of its members since the CDF report was issued.

Utilizing a three-day process of sustained prayer and dialogue, the assembly participants considered various responses to the CDF report, with the goal of deciding together on next best steps for the conference following the assembly. Recognizing that this is a time of historic challenge for the church and for LCWR, the participants expressed the hope of maintaining LCWR's official role representing US women religious in the Catholic Church. While acknowledging deep disappointment with the CDF report, the members proclaimed their intention to use this opportunity to explain to church leaders LCWR's mission, values, and operating principles.

The members charged the LCWR officers with beginning a conversation with Archbishop J. Peter Sartain, the apostolic delegate appointed by CDF to oversee LCWR. Their expectation is that open and honest dialogue may lead not only to increasing understanding between the church leadership and women religious, but also to creating more possibilities for the laity and, particularly for women, to have a voice in the church.

The assembly articulated its belief that religious life, as it is lived by the women religious who comprise LCWR, is an authentic expression of this life that should not be compromised. The theology, ecclesiology, and spirituality of the Second Vatican Council serve as the foundation of this form of religious life – and while those who live it must always be open to conversion – the life form should not be discounted.

The assembly instructed the LCWR officers to conduct their conversation with Archbishop Sartain from a stance of deep prayer that values mutual respect, careful listening, and open dialogue. The officers will proceed with these discussions as long as possible, but will reconsider if LCWR is forced to compromise the integrity of its mission.

The members reiterated the importance and value of LCWR's mission to its members and its role as a voice for justice in the world. They urged the officers not to allow the work with CDF to absorb the time, energy, and resources of the conference nor to let it distract the conference from the work its mission requires.

Appendix C

Joint Final Report

Following the publication of the Doctrinal Assessment of the Leadership Conference of Women Religious (LCWR) by the Congregation for the Doctrine of the Faith (April 18, 2012), the officers of LCWR and the Bishop Delegates began working in close collaboration toward the implementation of the Mandate which accompanied that document. From the beginning, our extensive conversations were marked by a spirit of prayer, love for the Church, mutual respect, and cooperation. We found our conversations to be mutually beneficial. In this Joint Final Report, we set forth the manner in which the implementation of the Mandate has been accomplished.

LCWR Statutes: The Statutes of the Conference were definitively approved for the first time by the Sacred Congregation for Religious in 1962; a revised text was subsequently approved by the Congregation for Institutes of Consecrated Life and Societies of Apostolic Life on June 29, 1989. LCWR had initiated a review of the Statutes prior to receiving the Mandate. In response to the 2012 Mandate, a subcommittee representing LCWR and the Bishop Delegates reviewed that document, attentive to the Mandate's request for greater clarity in expressing the mission and responsibilities of the LCWR as a Conference of Major Superiors under the ultimate direction of the Apostolic See. Through a collaborative process of mutual learning and of refining several drafts, it was agreed that "the role of the Conference as a public juridic person centered on Jesus Christ and faithful to the teachings of the Church is to undertake through its membership and in collaboration with other sisters those services which develop the life and mission of women religious in responding to the Gospel in the contemporary world" (Statutes, Section 2). At the conclusion of this drafting and refining process, the subcommittee's work was considered ready to be submitted to the LCWR Assembly. The 2014 Assembly overwhelmingly approved the text, and it was forwarded to the Apostolic See. Following a positive review by the CDF, the revised Statutes were approved on February 6, 2015 by Decree of the Congregation for Institutes of Consecrated Life and Societies of Apostolic Life.

Conference Publications and Programs: The Mandate also called for a review of LCWR publications to ensure that the Conference's mission would be fulfilled in accord with Church teaching. The Conference's mission is in service of its members and their positive role of collaboration in the Church's mission. At the same time, LCWR publications serve a larger audience in the Church. Many persons desiring spiritual growth have become readers of various publications. The nature of LCWR publications is intended to address spiritual matters rather than engage in formal theological inquiry. Nevertheless, because of the vital link between spirituality and theology, and in order to inspire, help evaluate experience as Women Religious, and challenge to growth, publications need a sound doctrinal foundation. To this end, measures are being taken to promote a scholarly rigor that will ensure theological accuracy and help avoid statements that are ambiguous with regard to Church doctrine or could be read as contrary to it. This exercise of theological responsibility is for the sake of both Conference Members and other readers. At the same time, it serves to protect the credibility of the Conference itself as a long-standing canonical entity of the Church. In addition, a publications Advisory Committee exists and manuscripts will be reviewed by competent theologians, as a means of safeguarding the theological integrity of the Conference.

The Mandate also addressed care in the selection of programs and speakers at General Assemblies and other LCWR-sponsored events. The choice of topics and speakers appropriate to the Conference's mission and service will be carried out in a prayerful, thoughtful and discerning manner. As with written publications, LCWR expects speakers and presenters to speak with integrity and to further the aims and purposes of the Conference, which unfold within the wider context of the Church's faith and mission. When a topic explicitly addresses matters of faith, speakers are expected to employ the ecclesial language of faith. When exploring contemporary issues, particularly those which, while not explicitly theological nevertheless touch upon faith and morals, LCWR expects speakers and presenters to have due regard for the Church's faith and to pose questions for further reflection in a manner that suggests how faith might shed light on such issues. As with publications, this kind of professional integrity will serve the Members well. Finally, a revised process for the selection of the Outstanding Leadership Award recipient has been articulated.

Other issues addressed by the Mandate: Over the past three years, considerable time and attention were given to dialogue regarding other matters raised by the Mandate, including the importance of the celebration of the Eucharist; the place of the Liturgy of the Hours in religious communities; the centrality of a communal process of contemplative prayer practiced at LCWR Assemblies and other gatherings; the relationship between LCWR and other organizations; and the essential understanding of LCWR as an instrument of ecclesial communion. These discussions had their origin in the Mandate and led to clarifying and fruitful conversation.

Conclusion: Our work together in response to the Mandate has borne much fruit, for which we give thanks to God and the gentle guidance of the Holy Spirit. The very fact of such substantive dialogue between bishops and religious has been a blessing to be appreciated and further encouraged. The commitment of LCWR leadership to its crucial role in service to the mission and membership of the Conference will continue to guide and strengthen LCWR's witness to the great vocation of Religious Life, to its sure foundation in Christ, and to ecclesial communion.

Most Rev. J. Peter Sartain
Archbishop of Seattle

Sr. Sharon Holland, IHM
LCWR President

Most Rev. Leonard P. Blair
Archbishop of Hartford

Sr. Marcia Allen, CSJ
LCWR President-Elect

Most Rev. Thomas J. Paprocki
Bishop of Springfield in Illinois

Sr. Carol Zinn, SSJ
LCWR Past President

Sr. Joan Marie Steadman, CSC
LCWR Executive Director

Appendix D

This facilitator guide provides an example of the many processes that LCWR created to use at gatherings of our members to assist all of us in discerning the movement of God in our lives -- individually and collectively. We share it as an idea for how a group may engage in communal discernment.

Guide for 'Behold, I am Doing Something New' Contemplative Process
(Created for a 90-Minute Time Frame)

The facilitator invites the participants to divide into groups of 5-7 and to form a circle with their chairs. A handout with questions for consideration is provided for each person. The facilitator leads the group through the process. The time allotted for each portion of this process is given merely as a guideline. The facilitator should adjust these times as appropriate to what is happening among the group.

The Contemplative Process

1 minute
Invite participants into a quiet space (breathe deeply, relax their bodies). Once people are settled, state: "Behold, I am doing something new... Can you not perceive it?" (Isaiah 43:19)

5 minutes
Invite the members to a quiet reflection.
Imagine yourself looking back since we began this gathering. As you move yourself through the various parts of this gathering, look back with no judgments, no questions, but rather just with a contemplative gaze.

3 minutes
Consider in quiet: What I hear emerging as a call to the conference is...

10 minutes
Each person shares with her small group: What question or reality may be emerging for LCWR?

1 minute
After listening to one another, in quiet, try to name for yourself what your small group feels is emerging.

10 minutes
What would your group name as one thing emerging that you would like to consider together?

10 minutes
As you think about what may be emerging, in quiet, consider these questions:
- What response does this reality call for from LCWR?
- Are you hearing anything these days that is influencing your perception about what is emerging? If so, how can you give greater attention to that influence?
- What do you believe LCWR is learning as it faces this reality?

20 minutes
Small group sharing on the responses to these questions.

1 minutes
As you think about your group's conversation, reflection, in quiet, ask yourself: Of all the insights shared in our group, what is the ONE insight that you feel your small group should share with the whole group? Not a synthesis – just a sharing of one of the insights.

10 minutes
Share your thoughts on what ONE insight you feel would be helpful to share with the whole. Invite the group listener/reporter to take notes and test out what that one insight is from your group.

10 minutes
Allow the small group listener/reporter time to compose her brief report and test it out with the rest of the group. What is the one insight your small group most wants to share with the rest of the board?

4 minutes (depending on the number of small groups)
Invite each small group listener/reporter to share her group's insight.

Closing
After participants take a brief pause to consider all that has emerged, the facilitator prays: We ask God to keep these hopes and desires present in our hearts as we close this time. We ask that we be open to participating in "the new" God may be wishing to create. Amen.

Gratitude to the Artists

We are profoundly grateful to the women religious who have given us permission to include their artwork in this publication. Their creations greatly enhance the communication of the messages and values that we hope this book conveys.

Doris Klein, CSA
p. 18

Mary Southard, CSJ
pp. 26, 44, 54, 82, 93, 132

Carol L. Smith, CSJ
p. 41

Jeanne Ambre, SSCM
p. 68

Margorie Thompson, SSJ
p. 107

Donna Korba, IHM
pp. 117, 143, 157

Made in the USA
Middletown, DE
29 April 2018